Dark Night
Journey

Dark Night Journey

Inward Re-patterning
Toward a Life Centered in God

Sandra Cronk

Pendle Hill Publications

Library of Congress Cataloging-in-Publication Data

Cronk, Sandra Lee, 1942–
    Dark night journey : inward re-patterning toward a life centered
in God / Sandra Cronk.
        p.   cm.
    Includes bibliographical references.
    ISBN 0–87574–914–3 : $12.50
    1. Spiritual life—Friends authors. 2. Spiritual formation-
-Society of Friends.   I. Title.
BX7738.C76 1991
248.2—dc20

                                        91–13925
                                          CIP

*To my parents
and my grandmother*

Contents

Introduction

One of the most powerful pathways in the journey to God is the time of stripping and emptiness called by many "the dark night." The name is apt. It describes the situation of those who have had a growing sense of relationship with God and are suddenly bereft of an experience of God's presence, direction, and consolation. Accompanying the loss of the experience of God is the unexpected opaqueness of all those areas of our lives through which God's light used to shine, giving meaning and purpose.

Just as a journey to a new location is full of confusion and misgiving when made in the blackness of a moonless night, so the nighttime spiritual journey is a bewildering occasion. Aridity, meaninglessness, loss, and pain are our most frequent companions, hardly the milestones we expect in a journey toward God—yet this is a journey toward God. The problem is that as we come closer to God we expect to be able to see our pathway more easily. Human experience over the centuries shows that this is not always the case. On the contrary, clear seeing is not at all as we had imagined it. This paradoxical journey in darkness is a time of God's powerful, albeit hidden, work in our lives. God's work in us occasions an intensive re-patterning of our whole being.

The reflections presented in this book come from travel-

ing this path myself and from listening to others who have
also come this way. Throughout the past decade I was a
teacher and community member at Pendle Hill, a Quaker
center for study and contemplation, near Philadelphia,
Pennsylvania. While there I had the privilege of hearing
many people share accounts of the way the Spirit moved
in their lives—healing, shaping, and guiding them. Numerous people spoke about experiences of radical stripping,
emptiness, and the absence of God. Although most of the
people had never heard of the phrase "dark night," their
experiences followed the pattern described by the writings
about this spiritual pathway. I discovered that such experiences are much more widespread than I had ever supposed.
The large number of these experiences took me by surprise.
In everyday circumstances we rarely talk about these times
in our lives. As a result, we don't have an accurate sense
of how frequent these experiences are. More importantly,
we don't know how others have tried to understand what
was happening during these times. We don't know how to
respond when we find ourselves or a close friend in the
same situation. This lack has caused many people over the
years to ask for help to comprehend what was happening
in a dark night, for help to know how to respond faithfully
to God when God seemed absent, or how to give a word
of encouragement to others.

This book grows out of these requests and out of the
yearnings, insights, and understandings that so many
people have shared over the years. It is written to help both
those who walk this journey and those who are spiritual
friends and nurturers of dark night travelers. The aim of
the book is to help readers understand this pathway: its
rootedness in Christ's crucifixion; its place as part of
apophatic mysticism. The aim is also to understand the

significance of some of the baffling experiences encountered along this dark night pathway: the new modes of
being with and knowing God which emerge on the journey; the possible hazards we confront; the importance of
the dark night for many of those facing severe illness and
death; the inward preparation for ministry wrought by
God during this journey; and the distinctive patterns of life
and ministry given to some who travel this way.

Cataphatic and Apophatic Pathways

Those who have looked at the history of Christian
spirituality or at the experience of their own lives realize
that we experience God's love in our lives through many
avenues (worship, reading Scripture, taking a walk in the
country, conversation with a friend, or the special closeness
that comes when reading the children a bedtime story). We
do not usually stop to analyze these different pathways.
Most of the time, it is not necessary. In the times that have
traditionally been called dark night, however, it can be
helpful to be aware of the extraordinary breadth of God's
work in our lives. We may be so used to a single way of
coming to God or of a few ways that God comes to us
that we are completely bewildered when those patterns
change, when God may be calling us to realize our lives
in deep communion with the One Divine Life. In the dark
night we come to recognize that our customary patterns
of knowing cannot begin to comprehend all that is God.

This book will explore briefly, in chapters 1 and 2, two
avenues that can help us recognize and acknowledge God's

work in our lives even in the midst of darkness: Scripture and the apophatic tradition. With these understandings as background, the remainder of the book will explore more fully the dark night experience itself and how it can help form persons and their communities. Two theological terms are of particular importance in these reflections: the cataphatic way (or *via positiva*) and the apophatic way (or *via negativa*). These terms have a long history of usage in religious thought.

The cataphatic path is that one in which God makes use of all the richness of our created world to touch our lives: our relationships with others, the meeting- and church-community, our jobs, the record of Scripture, our very ability to use language, images, and concepts in meditation, worship, and prayer. The list is almost endless. We probably have all had experiences of God's healing, comforting, discomforting, or guiding presence through one or more of these avenues.

We find ourselves in the apophatic pathway when words, images, and even our deepest relationships with others cannot hold or express all that God is. Ultimately, God is beyond all avenues of experiencing. The richness and full-ness of God's presence so overwhelms our limited capac-ities for expression that silence may sometimes seem more appropriate than any speech.

Both ways of "coming" to God or of God "coming" to us may issue in a deep mystical communion. Both form parts of most people's lives. They are two sides of the same reality.

Those who make a study of spiritual pathways point out that each of us has a relationship with God and a life in God that is expressed in a unique combination of these two intertwining strands. Some people may find one strand predominant all their lives. The other strand is like the underside of an embroidered cloth. It may be present, yet we do not always experience it in our everyday lives. Other people find that their predominant pattern may change with the passage of time, unfolding circumstance, and personal choice.

The dark night comes or can come to people who walk in any and all combinations of spiritual pathways. It can be expressed in cataphatic and apophatic language. The dark night is a time of preparation for a life lived more fully centered in God. In the stripping and emptiness, we discover that God bursts beyond all our previous avenues of knowing. It is a time of *not* knowing in one sense; and yet it is also a time of realizing that our life ultimately grows out of life with God. The dark night is a time of letting go of a more familiar way of encountering God. It may be a time when old understandings die, and new ones are born. Through these times, we may come to understand God, ourselves, and our world in a new way.

Most contemporary people are at home in the cataphatic pathway, even if they have not heard the technical term before. For example, a great deal of emphasis in contemporary spiritual-life literature grows out of the cataphatic awareness of God's presence in our everyday lives of work, family relationships, meditation, etc. We are accustomed to looking for God's presence in this way. Most people have had less experience with apophatic awareness. For this reason, the book will give an introduction to the apophatic path. Many people have found an understanding of the apophatic path helpful in interpreting their experience of absence and emptiness.

The full apophatic pathway is the contemplative tradition of Christianity. Exploring that pathway completely

would mean looking at diverse dimensions of our consciousness and awareness, mystical or contemplative experiences of unity, and modes of knowing and loving that
can approach the blazing darkness of the Divine. This
richness is clearly outside the limited intent of this book.
The book will explore only those dimensions of the
apophatic path that relate to the dark night.

Readers who would like to know more about both
cataphatic and apophatic pathways will find suggested readings in the bibliography. I only hope that the small glimpses
of each of the two pathways presented in this book will
help those who feel themselves in the midst of darkness to
know that God is in the mystery they encounter.

Cataphatic and Apophatic Experiences Come to Us All

Some readers may feel that these spiritual pathways are
outside their personal experience. I would like to suggest
that this is probably not the case. Most people have had
experience of both cataphatic and apophatic pathways. We
simply have not used the vocabulary to talk about them.
Those who are Friends or who have participated in a
Friends meeting for worship probably experience both
modes in worship.

Some observers have commented that the Friends mode
of spiritual life grows out of the apophatic tradition. In the
traditional Friends meeting for worship the worshipers
gather in silence, waiting upon the leading of the Spirit of
Christ. Out of the silence, any worshiper may offer a

spoken message or vocal prayer. We use no liturgy. We know no words or forms can convey all that God is and that created forms run the risk of idolatry. Our history has been one of iconoclasm—breaking old forms—both in worship and in the established ecclesiastical, social, and political structures of society.

In one sense, we have had an especially powerful apophatic dimension in our heritage. In another sense, this emphasis is only half of the picture. For example, early Friends issued a prophetic challenge to certain religious, political, and economic structures which they felt were unfaithful to God's call to justice and righteousness. At the same time, they formed new religious, economic, and social structures in their developing communities. In the same way, Friends worship manifests both cataphatic and apophatic dimensions. The silence in an unprogrammed meeting for worship is an open and receptive time. Worshipers may enter it in either spiritual mode. In fact, it is common for many people to begin with a cataphatic approach that stresses experiential relationship with God and other people. The worshiper may begin by saying an inward prayer for all of those gathered together, that each may find the healing and guidance she or he needs and that together they may come into God's presence. Thinking of God's work in her life, the worshiper may find it appropriate to begin a brief time of reflection on the past week. She may remember the times when God's presence touched her life, the places of inward struggle, the joys, and the burdens. Perhaps a particular burden needs to be lifted up to God (a loved one is ill) or a special thank-you uttered (in remembrance of that beautiful sunset or in gratitude that there has been food on the table in the midst of hard economic times). The person may choose or be inwardly given a passage from Scripture or from a favorite hymn that serves as a center for meditation. This passage, for example, may be on God's love. The worshiper becomes aware of a dimension of God's love that had been overlooked. One in worship may also feel that God is bringing this awareness to the whole meeting perhaps as part of a resolution to a dilemma the meeting has been facing, in which case she or he may give a vocal message to the meeting in this vein.

All of these aspects of worship might be considered part of the cataphatic mode of worship. We are grateful for the gifts that God brings to us through our relationships with others, our discursive meditations, the images of God's love and presence presented in Scripture, and so forth.

Also in the same meeting for worship, or the next one, the worshiper may come to an inward place where it seems right to lay aside, for the moment, all intercessory prayer, discursive meditation, and all reflections on God's work and the needs of those close to us and those far away. Perhaps one in worship senses, for example, that he is only going round and round in his mind about a problem, to no good point. He will and must take these things up again later, perhaps with new energy and insight. For the moment, however, it seems right simply to be in the quiet. The worshiper does not try to "do" anything, but simply to "be" in that which is eternal. It may be that vocal messages or his own thoughts bring him back to one of the cataphatic modes of worship. An insight about a problem, a sense of healing, or other helpful thought may arise. The worship period may then be a movement back and forth between the cataphatic and apophatic ways of being with and in God.

Messages may be given in the silence that do not bring worshipers back to self-defining thought or disturb the unitive awareness. In such circumstances the worship is more consistently in the apophatic mode. The worshipers are brought to a sense of oneness, although they may not even be aware of what is occurring or have any thoughts about it until they can reflect on it at the conclusion of the worship. On these occasions, one can often hear worshipers express surprise that the worship hour is ended so quickly. They are unaware of the passing time.

All of these ways of worship are treasured. The Quaker tradition has an expectation that worship will include all these dimensions. At the same time, Friends have been content to let God gather worshipers in whatever way may be best on each occasion, trying not to force the Spirit into one mode or the other. As a result, Friends have experience in diverse modes of worship, often without realizing it.

Those in other traditions can find parallels in their own heritages. Within Christianity, for example, certain spiritual disciplines emphasize these two ways of being with God. Centering prayer, sometimes called wordless prayer, is a discipline that grew out of the apophatic heritage, especially as it was practiced in monastic communities. This form of prayer is now widely used by those both within and outside monastic communities. Other prayer and meditational disciplines make use of images, Scripture passages, remembering, reflective thought, and other helpful aids. These usually reflect the cataphatic way. Of course, many prayer forms combine these approaches which, after all, are only our different ways of understanding one reality.

As we begin to think about our own experience, we can see that these spiritual paths are sometimes available to us through our choice. We can choose to follow one prayer form or meditational method. Other times, the choice is not really ours. It is simply given to us. Friends know this double-sided reality from their experiences in meeting for worship. There are days when it seems we choose to enter worship in a certain way. On other days we are taken into worship in a way that feels as though it comes from outside of our own choice. We learn very quickly that no matter what happens, we can in no way force God's presence by anything we do or do not do. God's presence is purely gift. We also learn that our "sense" of God's presence is not necessarily an indicator of whether worship has taken place. We may only know about God's work (presence, play) during worship at a much later time, and perhaps not even then. Much about these spiritual pathways remains beyond our control. Naming these pathways is not a way to gain any control over the spiritual life. Such control is impossible. The naming may only help us be more open and receptive to God's work. Letting go of the need to control our spiritual path is especially helpful in the dark night because in these times we do not choose a path. We experience the path as given. Walking in trust, along the path that is given, is our way of saying yes to God.

Exploring the Dark Night

Any discussion of the dark night must be limited in its intent. All parts of the spiritual journey are grounded in Mystery that surpasses our human knowing. This is especially true of the dark night. The times of darkness bring us face to face with our finitude and with the Mystery that is the ground of our being.

Fundamentally, there is no way to explain the dark night. We can, however, recognize it in our human experience. Those who have traveled this way can tell us a few of the landmarks in this unfamiliar terrain. When we feel lost and bewildered, there is comfort in knowing that others have come before us.

Paradoxically, accounts of other people's experiences or theoretical interpretations can also become hindrances for us, especially if we use them wrongly. For example, the historical accounts we have of dark night experiences often come from well-known figures whose lives are seen today as models in the religious life. When we hear that these famous people went through a dark night, we may feel that we are making some kind of spiritual progress if we can identify a similar experience in our own lives. Rather than being humbled under the cross, we are pleased with ourselves. Rather than turning more fully to God, we rely on our spiritual journey and the "progress" we feel we are making. Far from helping us turn to God, these accounts may feed our desire to provide our own salvation.

There is, of course, a rightful place for the use of our understanding. We are called to say yes to the movement of God in our lives. Our understanding of the ways in which God may move, helps us to say yes. The book is offered, in this context, as an aid to our understanding.

1

Dark Night in Scripture

Accounts of the dark night experience are at the center of the biblical records of God's work in history. The accounts of the Exodus and of Christ's crucifixion are perhaps the central experiences in the history of Israel and of the Christian church, respectively. Both follow what has come to be called in Christian spirituality the dark night pattern. People on a journey with God, who had made a deep faith commitment, suddenly were brought to a confrontation with death and darkness. God appeared to have deserted them. Instead of being closer to God and to the fullness of life they had anticipated, they felt as though God had forsaken them. Both of these occasions, however, were the very ones through which God was able to bring the people into a covenantal relationship of mercy and righteousness.

In the Exodus story, the pivot of the Hebrew Scripture, God led the Hebrew people out of slavery in Egypt to a new home in Canaan. The people were not able to enter directly into the Promised Land. Instead, they had to wander for forty years in the wilderness before they were able to inherit their new home. It was a time of darkness, failure, and constant stripping away of all humanly based power and strength. The people feared God had abandoned them, but in reality it was through this time in the desert that the people learned not to abandon God. The wilderness journey grew out of the people's confrontation with their fear and its consequences.

The Hebrew slaves had imagined that freedom from physical captivity would allow them to live as free people. But they discovered that they had brought their slavery with them. They were enslaved to fear.

> And they said to Moses, "Is it because there are no graves in Egypt that you have taken us away to die in the wilderness? What have you done to us, in bringing us out of Egypt? Is not this what we said to you in Egypt, 'Let us alone and let us serve the Egyptians'? For it would have been better for us to serve the Egyptians than to die in the wilderness."
>
> Exodus 14:11-12

The former slaves could hardly bring themselves to trek across the desert. They felt it would be better to turn back to the servitude they had known in Egypt than to suffer the anxiety and possible death involved in moving toward freedom.

Through fear the people became enslaved to a desire to control their own fate. They made a golden calf from their own jewelry (hence, from themselves). This god was under their control; they hoped it could grant their wishes. A golden calf can be very comforting when God seems far away, when we are stripped of all that is familiar, and when we doubt that any new home awaits us.

In such a state of mind and heart the Hebrew people were not able to enter the Promised Land. The prospect was too frightening. They did not know how to be free. They did not know how to be in trusting relationship with God who is the source of human freedom. They thought freedom meant to be autonomous, to be independent unto themselves. They needed to learn that being separated unto oneself only makes us a slave to our innermost fears and lusts. The only way out of this inner slavery is a relationship of trust with God.

This relationship of trust is what the Covenant on Mt. Sinai signified. God had become their God. But the people still did not know how to be God's people. They had to learn. The wilderness wandering, this season of repeated failure and renewed stripping, was their time of learning. Cut off from their humanly structured world, the people began to learn how to trust God. In the wilderness the people recognized that their food came from God. Their drink came from God. Their very survival came from God. Only as they gave up reliance on their own power did they come to trust God's faithful leading. Paradoxically, it was this detachment from their own power which made them strong enough to enter the Promised Land. The Israelites' wilderness journey was a dark night journey from slavery to freedom, from centeredness in self to centeredness in God.

At the heart of the Christian Scripture are the events of Jesus' crucifixion and resurrection. These events brought people face to face once again with that human enslavement which turns us away from God. The biblical account records just how difficult it was to live as a faithful people. Fears, angers, hurts, and lusts made them turn away from God. Even their religious observance had become a way of separating themselves from God and gathering the central power for their lives back into their own hands. So God again came to their aid. God sent One to free them and to enable them to live in the new order or kingdom of God. The climax of the drama for salvation (freedom and wholeness) came at the crucifixion and resurrection.

For those in the Christian faith, Jesus' death on the cross is rich in meaning. At the same time, it is a profound confrontation with darkness, failure, and emptiness which seems to overturn all meaning. It enables those within the faith to understand themselves and their relationship with God. It also points them toward divine mystery beyond human understanding.

By looking with the eyes of faith at the accounts of Jesus' life and crucifixion, Christians have traditionally understood that they and all people are in the same position as the slaves upon leaving Egypt. We all have become separated from God, from each other, and from ourselves. We no longer live as faithful followers of God. On the cross Jesus paid the penalty for our sin and unfaithfulness so that we can go forward, free of guilt and penalty, able to enter God's kingdom without the burden of the past preventing us from becoming the full, free human beings God has created us to be.

For Christians, the cross reveals more than the gift of freedom from the guilt and penalty of our unfaithfulness. It shows the extraordinary way God works in Christ to bring salvation and wholeness. It is the way of love, the way that gives up the use of coercive and manipulative power. Christ did not usher in God's new order through force of arms or through the use of political and economic might; indeed, the whole of Jesus' life was a manifestation of another way of being in the world, the way of the servant. He revealed that God works through another kind of power, the power of transforming love. At the cross Jesus remained faithful to God's love. He did not protect himself, his ministry, or his vision of God's new order with force. He lived and died with complete trust and dependence on God. Christ's life and death, in oneness with God, brought the gift of reconciliation and at-one-ment with God to his followers. The cross did not just remove the burden of personal sin; it opened the way to faithful living in God's new order. Christians in the early church understood themselves as people called to participate in and to manifest Christ's redemptive work. Their lives of servanthood, powerlessness in the world, nonviolence, and martyrdom presented a radical critique to the prevailing social order of that day, and of any day.[1]

The cross lies at the center of Christian faith with these profound layers of meaning. These rich layers, however, do not gather up all that is experienced in and through the cross. The crucifixion points toward a deep mystery which does not unveil itself to human eyes. The cross brings us face to face with that which we cannot fully understand: the death of God's son, the failure of Jesus' earthly ministry. The Prince of Peace received anger, hatred, and violence. The One who knew no sin received not universal acclaim but death. It was no imitation death. The cross was a complete stripping of any glory, power, knowing, and strength. It left only mockery, shame, loss of friends, and humiliation. Even God's presence was gone. Jesus experienced the emptiness of the dark night. "My God, my God, why hast thou forsaken me?" were the words upon his lips.

The cross, then, is a paradoxical revelation, a broken symbol. Symbols are supposed to open up meaning. Revelations, by definition, reveal. For the believer the cross does reveal much; yet it also points to the mystery of death,

---

[1]For a fuller understanding of the redemptive work of Christ on the cross, please see Sandra Cronk, *Peace Be with You: A Study of the Spiritual Basis of the Friends Peace Testimony*. Philadelphia: The Tract Association of Friends, N.D.

failure, and the absence of a God whom we can fully comprehend with our minds. The cross is an iconoclastic symbol which breaks open all human attempts to create our own salvation. We cannot become directors of our fate by possessing its meaning.

In Jesus' crucifixion we experience the failure of all human attempts to bring God's heavenly order on earth and to free ourselves from slavery and the consequences of our sin. As the ancient Hebrew slaves had to discard their humanly built calf in order to follow the true God, at the cross each of us must discard the last of our treasured expectations about the kingdom and our ability to bring it into being. Our trust must be in God, not in ourselves. At the center of the Christian faith is the place of darkness, emptiness, and unknowing where we are stripped of being our own rulers and our own gods and brought through Christ to God alone.

Through Jesus' faithfulness in the midst of failure and death, the world's reliance on self is shattered. Through his obedience, we are free to turn again to God. Each human being is now called to follow Christ on the path to the cross. We are called to die to the old life, to be crucified and stripped of all that is not of God. We enter the dark night of crucifixion to participate in Christ's life and death. In the darkness we discover that not we live, but Christ lives in us. Thus, we also participate in Christ's resurrection, God's gift of new life.

Christ's crucifixion re-orders the world. It is the central event which reaches back into earlier history and on into the future (our present and beyond), bringing all the world to God. We are part of that event. We enjoy its fruits, to be sure. But more than that, we participate in that event through Christ. To be followers of Christ means that the crucifixion two thousand years ago lives in us We also die and are given new life because we are one with Christ. We are transformed and re-patterned so that we may participate in the new order which creation is groaning to bring forth. We are part of that new birth, both as individuals and as a community of God's people. We are called to embody that new order in our social, political, and economic patterns of living. Through the crucifixion and resurrection, we are enabled to participate in Christ's redemption of the world. In that transforming dark night, we become like Christ, mirrors of God's love. We become able to love the world with God's healing, reconciling, and faithful love.

We experience this participation in Christ's crucifixion and resurrection in our daily lives and in worship. For many Christians the celebration of the Eucharist, communion, or Lord's Supper is a corporate way of giving meaning to personal dark night experiences and at the same time drawing the individual into God's eternal act of redemption in Christ's death and resurrection. In the Quaker heritage of unprogrammed worship there is no tradition of outward celebration of the sacraments. Accounts of Quaker worshipers from the earliest period to the present, nevertheless, indicate that the experience of inward crucifixion and resurrection is a central recurring element of the meeting for worship.

The experience of crucifixion is the dark night journey. In its pain, death, darkness, and emptiness, God gives, in Christ, resurrection and new life.

2

The Apophatic Tradition

Scripture presents an account of God's creating, sustaining, and redeeming work in history. Times of stripping and emptiness are a part of this record. In the scriptural accounts there is no explanation of dark night times; rather there are glimpses of meaning. Through such accounts, we do not so much understand all the mystery about God's relationship with us, but we are drawn more deeply into that relationship.

The dark night is so painful, in part, because it is hard to understand how that relationship can exist when all signs of the relationship appear to have been stripped away. All we experience is the absence of God. Two intertwining dimensions in our experience of our relationship with God help to explore more about the ways people have perceived their relationship with God, especially in times of emptiness and darkness; these are the cataphatic and apophatic modes of spirituality.

The cataphatic path (or the *via positiva*) recognizes that we enter relationship with God through all aspects of creation. We all have probably had experiences of coming to a deeper relationship with God through experiences with nature or through the caring of a loved one. We use our minds and our ability to think and reflect on our experiences in order to come to some, admittedly provi-

sional, understandings of God. Many kinds of prayer are
built on these possibilities. We may try to imagine ourselves
in a scene described in Scripture. We may meditate on the
meaning of the great truths of the Christian faith—the
incarnation, the cross, and the resurrection. We may reflect
on the ways God has touched our lives during the past
week. Through prayer and an attitude of open receptivity,
we may receive many indications that God is present in
our midst. We may have an overwhelming sense of being
loved. Perhaps a knot of hurt and woundedness begins to
unravel in our lives. We may have a strong sense of being
called to work toward social justice when we become
aware of a deep injustice in our community. We may receive
a strong inward or outward chastisement which we perceive as coming from God to soften a hardened place of
insensitivity within us. All of these are cataphatic ways of
experiencing our relationship with God. They are very
powerful. We can see why the term *via positiva,* affirmative
or positive way, is sometimes used to describe this path.
Through this path we can affirm God's relationship with
creation and the possibility of knowing God in and through
the created order.

This mode of spiritual understanding also takes seriously
the times of stripping and emptiness. The scriptural language about the wilderness wanderings and about the
crucifixion rests within this cataphatic framework. These
historical images of God's work help us to reflect on the
reality of the times of darkness and emptiness and on God's
work in these mysterious times.

The apophatic heritage (or *via negativa*), in distinction to
the emphasis of the cataphatic way, stresses that no words,
images, ideas, ideologies, or cultural expressions can gather
up all that God is. Revelation brings us to mystery. In

Exodus (33:20b) God tells Moses, " . . . for man shall not see me and live." God is beyond all our vision and thoughts. Our best attempts to explain and find expression inevitably fall short of the reality of God. Our experience of emptiness and absence is part of our encounter with that which is beyond our knowing. The apophatic heritage has taken a special interest in exploring the meaning of our encounter Beyond. This heritage has provided a rich basis for the expression of mystical life throughout Christian history. It has also been helpful in the specific expression of the spiritual journey often called the dark night. We will explore that part of the contribution of the apophatic heritage here.

Unfortunately, reflections about the apophatic heritage of Christian spirituality are not readily available to many people today, especially those outside the world of scholars. While streams within the Eastern Orthodox church, Roman Catholicism, and Quakerism have kept this heritage alive, for others (including many within these particular traditions) an understanding of the apophatic way has disappeared. To rectify that loss, this chapter will concentrate on reclaiming some of the understandings from the apophatic mode of spiritual expression that could be useful in understanding the dark night. At the same time, we will try not to lose sight of the contributions of the cataphatic heritage.

Two preliminary problems often create a distorted view of apophatic mysticism in the minds of twentieth-century people: 1) popular definitions of mysticism, and 2) contemporary assumptions about the nature of Christian faith and life. In order to see this heritage without distorted lenses, these problems must be faced and overcome.

To many people, the word mysticism conjures up an image of lights, voices, visions, or at the very least, deep insights about the nature of God and dramatic feelings of God's presence. Such experiences do occur. But they have nothing to do with the mysticism explored in the apophatic way. In fact, the mystics of this tradition have questioned the reliability of such experiences as the sole foundation for one's faith. They are aware of the conditioned character of all human experiences, whether it be a feeling of God's presence, a sense of direction, or the experience of consolation. Whether or not this awareness comes through a vision or through an inward feeling makes no difference. They proclaim that no human experience can claim to be an infallible mediator of God's presence or will. So mysticism for them does not rest on the existence of such special feelings or insights but, paradoxically, on the absence of them.

These mystics find God in the poverty and emptiness of our lives. More precisely, it is there God finds us. So mysticism in this tradition is plunging to the very depths and limits of what being human means, especially to those broken, empty places inside us. There we find even our religious ideas and assumptions shattered. Only then is it possible to enter into relationship with God. The popular, but limited, definition of mysticism must be discarded before trying to enter sympathetically into the apophatic way.

The second preliminary task is even harder. It requires that we step outside our own cultural assumptions to be able to see with fresh eyes. The apophatic way was very significant in understanding Christian prayer and spiritual life throughout most of the church's history. There have always been other forms of Christian spiritual life. In the last several hundred years a different cluster of emphases, values, and modes of knowing God has emerged as the predominant pathway of spiritual life. I call this cluster of meanings and assumptions the *via moderna* (modern way).

It has come to rival and, in many cases, to supplant apophatic understandings. With this transition to a new thought-world comes our problem. Most of us have been influenced by the *via moderna*. It colors our perception of ourselves, the world, God, and religious life.

The *via moderna* grows out of the cataphatic heritage, but it includes much more than a cataphatic emphasis. It incorporates a whole set of values and assumptions. This path is intensely this-worldly. It measures discipleship by activity, involvement with others, and working to change the world so that it manifests more fully God's love and justice. God is perceived in a this-worldly fashion as well. We believe God cares about our world and works in and through it. Jesus is God's Word incarnate. Christ has become one of us to reconcile us to God and to one another. Creation thus becomes the bearer of God, in a particular and special way through Christ, but in a more general way as well. God's redeeming love is often mediated to us through a caring friend or family member. God speaks to us in and through the natural world, relationships with other people, and events in our daily lives.

The *via moderna* is not simply the way of activity as opposed to the way of contemplation. It may also have a strong mystical orientation. But the mode of knowing God is very different from that of the apophatic way. In the *via moderna*, in keeping with its cataphatic roots, we know God in and through our experience. A sense of God's presence, direction, consolation, and chastisement may come to us through a variety of experiences. In this tradition, the experience of God's love and presence is a profound undergirding of one's faith and of one's service in the world.

All of this is real and true. The point is not to bring these understandings into question but to note how basic these assumptions are to our perception of Christian life and faith. This cluster of understandings is so central that we barely recognize that there are other dimensions of Christianity which have been important in generations past. Many of these other dimensions are reflected in the apophatic tradition. The apophatic way emphasizes those qualities which are the underside of the *via moderna*. In the apophatic way, being is more important than doing; relationship with God is primary; God is understood to be at work most profoundly when an experience of God's presence is absent; and living in the end-time takes precedence over trying to change the world through intensive political, economic, or social action.

All of these qualities together are perceived today as other-worldly. In fact, the term "other-worldly" itself is one of derision. A faith that concentrates on realities beyond this world is seen as irrelevant and mistaken in its understanding of the basic Christian message. Each of these apophatic emphases, however, is relevant to our daily living. Together they bring a prophetic critique to some of our unexamined assumptions from the *via moderna*.

What is the prophetic quality of each of the emphases mentioned above? The stress on being rather than doing is a recognition that doing Christ-like actions must come from being a Christ-like person. At a time of crisis or decision we are not going to choose to perform a Christ-like action if we have not become people of faith, trust, and love. Faithful doing is not ignored in the apophatic tradition; rather, the ground of that doing is more fully explored.

In the same way, the relationship with God is primary but not in the sense that relationship with other people is ignored. Charity is always the fruit of Christian faith. Our relationship with God, however, is the ground out of which our love and unity flourish. Moreover, our relationship with God is primary because it will continue throughout eternity, long after our time on earth is finished. Our relationships with others will exist in and through our communion with God. In this tradition, eternity is taken as seriously as life in time.

The apophatic stress on the absence of "experience" of God is not meant to imply that God does not or cannot give an experience of presence, direction, comfort, and chastisement in meditation, prayer, or in our daily life. These experiences may be very powerful. But the apophatic way recognizes that our experience is as finite and fallible as is our human nature. We may misunderstand what we experience. We may distort what we perceive through both conscious and unconscious processes. Of course, distortion may be corrected through proper discernment and judgment. This tradition reminds us, however, that in the best of circumstances no experience can capture the infinite. We should beware of assuming that it can. Perhaps even more important than these warnings is the recognition that even when such sensible experiences are absent, God may still be at work powerfully in our lives.

Finally, the apophatic tradition's stress on living now as though it were the end-time (rather than building the new order of God through religio-political action) has its root in a strong eschatological emphasis. Eschatology is the discipline which deals with the last days, with the millennium, with God's coming kingdom, which will displace life as we have known it on this earth.

Some Christians reject any interest in such themes because of the simplistic way in which some enthusiasts predict the coming of the kingdom—two o'clock in the afternoon of a given Friday—or because of poorly constructed attempts to match the imagery of the Book of Revelation with certain events in present political history. A dismissal of such themes, however, dismisses Jesus' ministry, which centered on the coming new order as a real event in our lives. Moreover, eschatological emphasis is itself a form of prophetic protest to a world fraught with injustice, oppression, separation, and alienation.

The heavenly kingdom is always emerging in our midst, challenging the structures of evil and unfaithfulness in the present order. We are always being called to enter a new way of life. This call comes as a judgment on our personal lives and on society as a whole. To continue on our present path leads to death, both because of the inherent consequences of our present lifestyle (e.g., proliferation of warfare and the threat of nuclear holocaust or the continued pollution of our planet and the destruction of our environment) and because of God's judgment.

God's kingdom is both a future historical and cosmic reality and an eternal reality already impinging on our world of time, bringing prophetic judgment and hope. To choose to live that end-time now is to choose to live in God's new order which overcomes the structures of injustice and the experiences of alienation and separation. Peace witness, communal ownership of goods, and the use of silence and celibacy have all been expressions of life in the end-time for various religious communities. The choice to live in the end-time is itself a testimony against those unfaithful structures of our present society. But the choice also recognizes that in the ultimate sense we do not build God's new order (although it takes shape and form through our faithful actions). Fundamentally, the kingdom is God's gift. We are invited to participate in that new order which is coming and come.

To choose to live in the end-time is also a witness to the fact that our life in this world is rooted in God's kingdom which extends beyond time. We know that all things in this world pass away. They are transient. To live now as though we were in that eternal order is to transcend the narrow boundaries of self, death, and time. The dark night journey is toward the death of the narrow, constricted concept of self. It is a moving out beyond self to the self which lives eternally in God, both in time and beyond time.

Early monastic communities in the Christian church which followed the apophatic way lived as though they lived now in that kingdom which was to be fully realized at the end of time. They recognized that in a real way, eternity had broken in on this world of time. And the values of the eternal world superseded those of this world; thus, they lived as celibates because none is given in marriage in that eternal world. They also understood that the ethics of the Sermon on the Mount gave structure to their monastic communities. They refused to accept the view that the Sermon on the Mount was an idealized ethic impossible to live in the real world. The result was not irrelevance, but a prophetic call to a society to live the way of love in recognition that the eternal kingdom, God's new order, is breaking in on our world.

In the apophatic tradition believers live an inverted life. Their roots are in the future, in the eternal world which is impinging on this world, constantly breaking open the narrow focus of our vision on earth. In contemporary society we tend to live entirely in this world. We measure all things by what happens here and now. When one lives only in this dimension, to talk only about chronological roots makes sense. Our roots are embedded in what went before, not in the reality of what is to be and what is already being born. It takes conscious reflection for us to be able to enter the thought-world where eternity is a present reality and where all structures are measured according to the values of God's inbreaking new order.

Thus, the other-worldly emphases of the apophatic tradition have much to say to this world and our lives here and now. In fact, the apophatic way and the cluster of values that make up the *via moderna* often have most relevance when they intertwine in the lives of individuals and communities. This intertwining is similar to melody and counterpoint in music. Both must sound if the fullness of the music is to be heard. Without the cataphatic emphasis, the apophatic way runs the risk of becoming contentless, separated from God's work in the Christ of history, and removed from the immediate needs of flesh-and-blood people. Without the apophatic way, the cataphatic has the danger of idolatry and confining God to our narrow ideas, concepts, and images. In our day, because of the general rootedness in the *via moderna* with its strong cataphatic emphasis, we need the apophatic way as a prophetic corrective.

Iconoclastic Language

The *via negativa* or apophatic way is an iconoclastic tradition which breaks open the limited images and categories we ordinarily use with symbols which point beyond the finite. For example, it is common to talk of God by identifying those qualities of human life which we have experienced on a higher plane in our relationship with God. We say God is loving, merciful, just, and powerful. These terms give us important understandings of God. They gather up much that is true in God's relationship with us. It is also true to our understanding to say that God is so far beyond our words, with their limited, finite meanings, that words cannot begin to describe God. The apophatic heritage breaks open such limited imagery. Instead it speaks with an unusual cluster of "negative" images (hence, the term, *via negativa*). This path, at first glance, may seem a denial of the God we know but, on closer inspection, it is really a denial of the use of limited imagery applied to God. These images of negation describe a new way of knowing God.

Images from the Apophatic Way	*Images from the* Via Moderna
Silence	Words
Emptiness	Fullness
Absence	Presence
Darkness	Light
Unknowing	Knowing
Virginity/ celibacy	Marriage/ human completeness
Poverty	Riches
Contemplation	Meditation
Solitude	Community

The apophatic writers speak more about silence as an avenue to God than the use of words; emptiness and absence are more characteristic of their encounters with God than fullness and presence; darkness is more usual than light; contemplation than meditation; unknowing than knowing. Even the way of life is turned upside down.

Poverty is more likely to be a discipline and a fruit of this way of life than riches; virginity is more common than marriage; solitude is emphasized instead of community.

These strange words of negation seem meaningless at first glance. What can it possibly mean to know God through emptiness and darkness? Why should one lift up such alternative patterns of living as voluntary poverty and solitude? What does unknowing mean? The answers to these questions are not esoteric, only to be understood by an elite few. They can be understood by all.

The first level of meaning comes out of awe for the God who transcends or is beyond all our human categories of thought. In fact, our human categories are in danger of becoming idols or pillars. We lean on these narrow images or ideas and believe we know God. These idols must be smashed before we can know the God who is behind our narrow idea of "god."

The language of the apophatic tradition, however, does not intend to make only a theological point about the nature of God. The language is experiential. It grows out of universal human experience. Most people can find at least part of their own experience expressed more fully by this language of negation than the "positive" language we are more used to using.

Language of Experience

The experiential dimension of the language of negation may be felt psychologically or emotionally in two different ways. One path is the gentle way which often comes through the practice of a chosen spiritual discipline (or sometimes as unexpected gift). It does not necessarily involve any perceived outward or inward stripping, which is part of the classical definition of the dark night. (Of course, the act of stripping away is seen very differently anyway when it is a voluntary part of an accepted religious discipline.) The second path involves the more painful and bewildering experience of involuntary loss. The term dark night is applied to the latter circumstance. We all can find ourselves walking in these two pathways from time to time.

Gentle Way—The gentle path is taken when, by gift or chosen spiritual discipline, we are able to give attention simply and easily to the encounter with God which arises in the emptiness rather than to anything which we may see as "missing," "taken away," or "given up." Sometimes the very language of negation may turn our attention to what is missing (God's presence, direction, comfort, or our own self-defining thoughts). Our attention, however, need not be directed in this way. We may, on occasion, simply be open and receptive to experience which is not defined by the content of awareness. It is "empty" of self-defining thoughts or analytical judgments about the elements of our world. This may leave us free to fall through to another level of awareness. Sometimes this happens more by "chance" or by pure gift than by any planning on our part. A quiet walk in the woods or by the seashore has often been the outward circumstance surrounding such an experience beyond usual thought. When least expecting it, we are in a state of open awareness, in which we are not conscious of the content of thought. We are simply one with all that is around us. In this "empty" inward place, we can meet God in a new way.

Sometimes we enter this same open or empty awareness through the use of a spiritual discipline. The discipline helps us enter that place of open and receptive awareness. Some examples may be useful. I shall choose some illustrations from the tradition with which I am most familiar, the Quaker heritage. Talking over the years with people from other traditions gives me confidence that readers will find parallels in their own situation even if their heritage is one with seemingly different structures of worship and polity. (For example, while acknowledging that there are important differences between times of personal prayer and corporate worship, those who are not Quakers may find that their experiences in individual silent prayer parallel, in significant ways, those of Friends in their unprogrammed meetings for worship.)

The Quaker tradition incorporates an apophatic discipline in its unprogrammed or silent meetings for worship. It is customary for some worshipers to enter the silence in quiet openness and receptivity with no attempt to think about or reflect on any aspect of their life or even their relationship with God. The attention is not on any thoughts (which may or may not continue to flow through the mind), but simply on allowing oneself to be, aware that the ground of that being is God. In this manner of worship, the fullness of God's presence may flow into spoken prayer and vocal messages. It may also transcend the capability of words to convey. Silence may then become an eloquent testimony to God.

The Quaker use of silence illustrates two central qualities about the symbols of the apophatic way. (1) They point us toward a place "behind" or "beyond" all of our thinking and doing, an "empty" place in the center of our human experience through which God can enter into relationship with us. When we symbolically fill ourselves with our own meaning, our own doings, and our own thoughts, there is hardly any place in our lives where God can encounter us. (2) The encounter with God brings us into relationship with One who cannot be captured entirely through words, concepts, images or forms; thus, language gives way to silence as symbolic expression. On one level silence says nothing. On another it gathers up all that might be said and more. It brings us to eternity where the Word of God is spoken beneath all words. Symbols from the apophatic way speak of a pathway to God, and they describe the encounter with God found in that pathway.

A word of caution may be in order here. The term "gentle way" to describe the path of voluntarily chosen apophatic disciplines may be a misnomer. Following any spiritual discipline with integrity and consistency is likely to produce its own hard times and struggles as we are brought to confront those sinful and broken places in ourselves which block us from loving God and others. Apophatic disciplines are no exception. Understanding this reality, it is nevertheless helpful to know that this gentle openness to God in quietness is an ongoing dimension in many people's spiritual journeys. This possibility is available to all of us.

The Quaker tradition is not only apophatic. While apophatic language captures some elements of Quaker experience, cataphatic language captures others. Most traditions have their own unique way of intertwining both spiritual pathways. Following the cataphatic mode, Friends place great stress on experiencing the presence of God in worship, on listening to Christ as the inward teacher, on receiving divine direction, comfort, healing, and chastisement, and on being gathered together as a people of God. They use the cataphatic disciplines of remembering, reflection, and imaging prayer as part of their discipline in worship. From this perspective, the silence provides the open space for our listening and response to Christ's work in our midst.

Spiritual disciplines from this cataphatic aspect of the Quaker heritage may also bring us to that place of emptiness and darkness. Indeed, disciplines which are not seemingly directed in any special way toward awareness of God in darkness, emptiness, absence, and loss may, in fact, be powerful teachers of the *via negativa*. For example, life in a community of commitment is a central spiritual discipline for Friends. It is very easy to expect that adherence to the meeting's expectations about caring and nurturing one another will inevitably bring a lovely, warm sense of support and encouragement in our daily lives together. We assume that a community committed to faithful living will manifest all those qualities we believe are part of Christian life. Of course, there are many wonderful things about a life lived together under Christ as teacher. One of the most powerful is that the community itself becomes a stark revealer of truth. In community we soon come up against all kinds of experiences that challenge our own ego-definitions. People do not concur with our notions of what is right and good. We realize that many do not agree with us about what faithfulness means. These problems are made more intractable because we respond to them out of fear, anger, frustration, and all the wounded places in our own lives.

We soon discover that there is no way to build our image of the loving, faithful community out of our own strength. We are brought humbly to a sense of emptiness, darkness, absence, and loss. Paradoxically, it is often then that we turn, in our weakness and repeated failure, to God. In this unexpected *via negativa* we encounter God beyond all our utopian thoughts, ideologies, or culturally limited expressions of appropriate church life. Only then does it become possible for us to accept God's gift of life in community.

Inasmuch as all of these spiritual disciplines, apophatic or cataphatic, help turn us to God, their pathways may intertwine. Disciplines which had at first seemed very disparate are in fact closely related. In this last example of choosing and living through a spiritual discipline, we come closer to that which comprises the dark night path rather than the gentle way. We see that our act of voluntarily choosing a discipline may bring us to the experience of the dark night which is traditionally perceived as given or even imposed.

The Dark Night Journey—The second way many people experience one dimension of the apophatic way is the dark night journey. On this pathway we do not slip easily into that open and receptive place beyond words. By definition, this path is not initially a voluntary or chosen one, although we may come to say yes to God in the midst of this rugged and painful way. At the beginning there is no intentional apophatic spiritual discipline. There is no gentle gift of contemplative awareness; instead we feel stripped until there is only absence and emptiness left.

This is the pathway of crumbling pillars, those finite supports on which we have based our life and our relationship with God. We are used to experiencing God in and through the created world. We find the meaning of God's love expressed in the love of a spouse, family, and friends. We have established ways of understanding the direction and purpose of our lives: in our jobs, church work, care for others, etc. Our world has a certain structure and order. We glimpse the divine through God's gifts of admonition, consolation, and direction in this order. All of this is good. God does work in these ways.

But what happens when the pillars of our lives begin to crumble? We face the death of a dear one; marriage ends in divorce; the economy slows down and our job disappears; the doctor announces we have a debilitating illness; a clear look at the international situation reveals that nuclear holocaust is not only a remote possibility but a growing probability; our beloved church community forsakes the ways we have always seen as signs of faithfulness, believing itself to be more relevant to the modern world; advanced age brings extreme frailty and loss of ability to take care of ourselves, or we discover that our membership in a dispossessed minority group will probably entail poverty and frustration throughout our entire lives. Suddenly our nicely ordered world can fall apart into meaninglessness. Not just the emotional shock of a particular tragedy strikes us. Along with the shock we discover that those pillars which we used to feel were so strong as manifestations of God's love and purpose are taken away. We discover that our very way of perceiving God has disappeared as well. All we experience now is darkness, emptiness, and meaninglessness. There is no place to turn for help. All the finite things we used to cling to are now revealed to be incapable of bearing the weight of the infinite. If we do not have these pillars, how do we know God? How does life have meaning? We are left in confusion.

Not only traumatic events may cause this radical upheaval in us. Sometimes it comes unawares, with no great outer changes. The old ways of prayer no longer seem to bring us closer to God. Meditations and devotional readings bring no sense of God's presence. Participation in the church, family, or job no longer conveys God's purpose in our lives. The sense of absence and emptiness is as great with these inner changes as in any situation of outward loss.

The apophatic language of darkness and emptiness may be very close to the experience of dark night journeyers in a variety of circumstances. This language is not just a conceptual system about the nature and limitation of human language. Consequently, many people find it helpful both in providing them with a way to express their experience and to understand how God may be at work in their lives when all the heretofore customary signs of that work are missing. It helps them to begin to see beyond what may have been the old avenues for knowing God.

Dark Night: Part of All Spiritual Pathways

For some people the dark night is a temporary, sometimes recurring, part of a broader spiritual pilgrimage which receives nurture largely through the "positive" symbols of the cataphatic mode. For these people, their first encounter with the path of emptiness may be in the dark night. Taken in the context of a person's whole life, the dark night may be seen as a counterpoint to another primary melody. Indeed, even in the midst of the dark night itself there are usually periods of light and the gift of the experience of God's presence. Such times of respite are great aids to those who must continue on this path.

For others, however, the apophatic way is the major pathway of the spiritual life. They are drawn to a contemplative form of life. For these people the dark night period of stripping is but one part of the total journey. The mode through which they encounter God, both during the dark night and afterwards, is in the apophatic manner (i.e., through the iconoclastic symbols of silence, darkness, and emptiness).

In the midst of our experience of darkness and crucifixion, apophatic and cataphatic language can help us to move into deeper relationship with God. The apophatic language points us Beyond. The cataphatic language, among other things, points us to the mystery of God's transforming work in the midst of the wilderness wanderings of the former slaves and the crucifixion of Jesus. Dark night occasions can and do come to us all, no matter what spiritual pathway seems to be our primary home.

What the Dark Night is Not

The phrase dark night journey is not intended to describe the situation of those who have not yet become aware of God's call in their lives or those who are unsure whether there is a God and are just beginning to search out an answer to that question. The phrase does not address the person who has lost sight of God through negligence. It does not speak to the condition of a person who does not reflect on God's work in his or her life all week long but then wonders why God seems silent during the one hour

given over to worship. In the same manner it does not deal
with the person who consistently refuses to answer when
Jesus stands at the door of the heart and knocks and then
wonders why the knocking eventually ceases. All these
people may experience a sense of emptiness, but the causes
are different.

The dark night describes the situation of those who have
had a growing sense of relationship with God and are
suddenly bereft of God's presence, direction, and consolation. This unexpected change can be devastating. Our
reaction is usually to flee from the emptiness to find some
sense of meaning again. We search for something to fill the
void. We try harder to engage in all the old pursuits and
types of prayer. We attempt new techniques of prayer or
search for new activities to give life meaning. We assume
that we can manipulate ourselves, the world, and even God
to bring meaning into our lives again. We believe we can
force the answers to our questions if we try hard enough.

Unlike other occasions in our life, when more initiative
on our part did yield new openings, this darkness does not
give way before our pressure. It only becomes more intense. The old forms of prayer do not "work." Instead of
God's presence, we experience only absence. All that we
may have lost remains lost: a loved one, health, a job. In
their place seems to be nothing. All that we had known
before is now taken away. This is a time of great stripping.
All those places we had looked to for our security and
meaning are gone. All that had given us a sense of personal
achievement has disappeared. There is only an empty space
inside and outside us.

Helpful Writings

To find oneself confronting this empty place may be frightening and painful. To know that others have walked this way before us and found new depth and meaning in their lives as a result can be enormously comforting. Some of these earlier journeyers have left accounts of their experiences and word-maps of the interior terrain they traversed. A familiarity with some of these accounts can be of great help both to a journeyer in the dark night and to spiritual nurturers who work with these interior travelers.

Two kinds of writings in the apophatic tradition are especially important for understanding the dark night journey. The first describes the psychological experience of this pathway and explores some of the deep re-patterning which goes on within us during this time. John of the Cross, a sixteenth-century Spanish Carmelite, is the recognized master of this kind of apophatic writing. His work, *Dark Night of the Soul,* is the classic description of this journey. Some Friends' journals are also rich in dark night imagery. Many writings from first-generation Friends and from the so-called quietist era of Quakerism are spiritual treasures because of their insightful portrayals of this inward stripping and of God's re-patterning of their lives. Two fine contemporary sources from outside the Quaker tradition are Carlo Carretto's *Letters from the Desert* and Thomas Merton's "A Philosophy of Solitude" in *Disputed Questions*. The second kind of writing is epistemological. Epistemology is the discipline which deals with how we know what we know. Such a discipline may seem remote from the immediate needs of the spiritual life. But, in fact, it is central because what is happening on this journey, along with the re-patterning, is the development of a different way of knowing God. The Christian tradition calls this different way of knowing contemplation or contemplative prayer. The anonymous writer of the fourteenth-century English classic *The Cloud of Unknowing* provides a superb description of contemplative prayer.

Both sets of writings ground their understandings in the experience of a deepened relationship with God which emerged in and through darkness and emptiness.

3

Dark Night

Being Re-patterned by God

Those who have traveled in the dark night have both very daring and, at the same time, very practical advice to give to new journeyers. "Stay in the darkness and emptiness. Do not flee from the nothingness or try to fill up that hollow place with your own attempts to create new finite pillars on which to build your life." The prescription is daring because it flies in the face of our instinct, as journeyers, to clutch at any straw in this dreadful time. It also contradicts the model for helpers of those in pain. Helpers wish to rescue, to fix all problems, and to make sure everything comes out all right. But rescuing is not in order here. God is to be found in the darkness, not away from it. Moreover, rescuing is not possible anyway. There are no more straws to clutch; there are no solutions to our dilemma; thus, the advice to stay in the emptiness is purely practical. There is no other choice. There is no way to prop ourselves up unless we are willing to settle for what we know are weak supports which will crack when we try to place any weight on them.

By facing the darkness, we confront that empty place inside each of us. That place marks the end or limit of all the finite things in creation, including the limit of ourself.

Our strivings after meaning and purpose—indeed, after God—have brought us to the end of ourselves and our own ability to encompass God. As we stand at the edge of these limits, we face nothing, or so it seems. But, paradoxically, just at this point when we face nothing, rather than ourselves or any other elements of creation, we may come to know our creator. In that empty place we can at last know that which transcends ourselves. We realize that in our relationship with God in the past we have turned more to God's gifts than to God alone. We have looked for comfort or challenge. We have looked for direction and meaning. These are fine and good, but now God brings us beyond those divine gifts. We come to God alone. We have, in the past, confused God's gifts with God. Now we begin to move beyond this confusion.

We begin to recognize a deeper conversion or turning to God which takes place in the dark night. A profound re-patterning begins in us. The re-patterning can happen because the old structure of our lives has been broken up. All those good but creaturely pillars will no longer serve as the center of our lives. Now that they are taken away, a new center can emerge. That new center is God. This new center is not simply an intellectually or emotionally based faith in God. The dark night journey has re-shaped our activity patterns, our value system, and our whole being so that God is the functional center of our living.

The apophatic way does not demean God's work in the natural world, our relationship with friends and loved ones, or our service and ministry in God's created order. The dark night journey does not take us to a place where we ignore these natural elements of human life. Rather, it allows us to see where we have inappropriately invested our faith, security, and trust in that which is created rather than in the One who underlies all creation. In the stripping of the dark night we encounter God in a deeper way than we may ever have allowed ourselves before.

For this deeper encounter to occur, two particular pillars of misplaced faith must be stripped away. They are the hardest supports to give up since we often do not even recognize them for what they are—false sources of security. These two pillars are our "self" and "god."

It is odd that we treat our "self" as if it were like any other finite thing we possessed and could control. We spend most of our lives trying to make ourselves more loving, more integrated, more humble, or better adjusted. Spoken about in such a bald way, the inner contradiction in our scheme is obvious. How can we use our "self" to overcome our "self"? But what is obvious logically is not experienced as such until we begin the dark night journey. To manipulate ourselves in this way is impossible. The outward elements of our life which used to bring a sense of fulfillment are often gone or drained of meaning. The techniques of prayer which used to be so meaningful are no longer so. We cannot control God's presence. In fact, our "self" has no material with which to work. As a result we feel as if that self has been broken.

In a deep sense, this is just what has happened. As the old self cracks open, we discover not the annihilation we had feared but a deeper "I." This deeper "I" is not a possession that can be remade through all our efforts at self-improvement. This deepest self is a gift from God. Recognizing that we exist because of God's gift of ourselves makes a new structure possible in our lives. Having let go of the self as a possession, we are able to let go of others as possessions or as "things" which touch us only insofar as they impinge on our efforts to make ourselves. Our love for others now springs from the awareness that others are also gifts of God. Our love does not come from our efforts to make ourselves more loving and caring by dint of our own ego-centered struggles. The journey which may have looked at first as though it were distancing us from other people and from the needs of this world has brought us to an inward place where we can love others with new depth because we are no longer the center of our own loving.

Miraculously, with the movement to a deeper center in our lives, we are able to release our hold on God as a possession. It may never have occurred to us that we had been treating God as a possession. This was the effect, however, when our relationship with God grew out of that former manipulative, possessive self. We had wanted a clear sense of direction and purpose. We had wanted comfort in times of distress. We had wanted the fruits of a close relationship with God, but we did not necessarily want God.

The problem, in fact, was even more deeply rooted. Previously we wanted God to enter our lives. We wanted to be more faithful. We wanted to be closer to God. In short, "we" had wanted everything. "We" wanted to be more faithful. "We" wanted to be closer to God. We wanted to do it all. We wanted to control that which gave meaning and power in our lives. In truth, we wanted to provide our own salvation. We wanted a god who would be yet another finite pillar under our control, a god that would take away the terror of facing that empty place which lurked at the limit of all finite things and at the end of our "self."

In the dark night, that god dies as our narrowly manipulating self dies. More accurately, we recognize that this god has never been there at all, except insofar as we have conjured up such a security blanket. At that moment a new encounter is possible with God who has been waiting in the darkness

from which we have been fleeing. For the first time there is
a substantial shift in focus. We recognize that it is not that
our lives need to be opened to God. This imagery comfort-
ably retains us in control; "we" allow God to enter "our"
domain. Now we recognize that God invites us into the
divine life. On the deepest level our existence has meaning
not because we let God into a lesser or greater piece of our
lives but because we are given life and love in God's life and
love. God's graciousness is such that we have received many
rewards in the past for our endeavors to open ourselves to
God. In the dark night, however, we discover that God is
not willing to settle for such bits of movement which do not
change the essential structure of relationship with God. In
the dark night, the structure itself changes.

This transformation marks our participation in Christ's
crucifixion. In the darkness all reliance on our human
efforts to bring salvation is shattered. The old self dies.
Into emptiness God brings new life. "I have been crucified
with Christ; it is no longer I who live, but Christ who
lives in me" (Gal. 2:20a). Our life becomes transparent to
the eternal Word, Christ.

New Way of Knowing God

The intensive re-patterning of our inward lives is not the only thing that happens in the dark night journey. It is also a time of learning to know God in a new way. The "knowing" is so bewildering and so unlike what we have come to expect that one classical work calls it "unknowing."[1] Those who enter this new way of knowing God continue to use the language of the *via negativa* or apophatic way to describe what they encounter because the journeyers are now looking beyond the limits of self, beyond the gifts of God to God alone. That means looking into that empty place. Here the language of the finite world is not able to comprehend the infinite. Iconoclastic imagery of the apophatic tradition becomes descriptive of the experience of seeing our affirmative theological categories broken open and our usual knowledge about God transcended by the reality of our relationship with God. Words such as emptiness, absence, and darkness express more clearly what the journeyer encounters than do words about presence and light. This shift in knowing happens naturally in our experience. It can, however, appear esoteric and complicated when explained in conceptual language. It is not that the conceptual language is so difficult but rather that the process being described is one of moving beyond conceptualization.

One way to understand the difference in the two modes of knowing is to recall the difference between analytical knowledge and a more holistic, relational knowledge. Our usual way of knowing depends on analytical and descriptive language that presupposes a distance and separation

---

[1] The anonymous fourteenth-century English classic, *The Cloud of Unknowing*.

between the knower and object known. This knowing is a "knowing about" an object, person, occurrence, or idea. I know about the chair in my room because I see its size and color. I can feel its hardness. I often know other people in this way, i.e., I know about them: their names, their physical attributes, their occupations, their habits. I know God in this way, too. Of course, I cannot describe God's physical attributes. I do know something about God, however, because I know what God has done in my own life, in the life of the church, and in the biblical history of the people of God. I know the leadings, consolations, and chastisements that have come to me from God. This is very helpful. It is a necessary way of knowing God. But it presupposes the same analytical relationship between me as the knower and God as the known as it does between me and my chair or the people I see passing my home.

When we are careful in our theology, we are not accurate to talk about God as one other thing to be known in a world of things. For all the items of creation have their being in God. God is not a thing or a being to be found in some otherwise unoccupied corner of creation.

On the dark night journey our knowing of God shifts in two ways. First, we encounter God as the source of our being and continued sustenance. "In him we live, move and have our being" (Acts 17:28a). We shift from knowing things about God's activity in the world to a deep communion with God. We are so close to God that the analytical dimension of our faculties does not operate, or its operations cease to be of primary importance. Thomas Merton describes this different mode of knowing when he writes about a hermit who travels the apophatic way.

> So great is his poverty that he does not even see God; so great are his riches that he is lost in God and lost to himself. He is never far enough away from God to see Him in perspective, or as an object. He is swallowed up in Him, and therefore so to speak, never sees Him at all.[2]

To the analytical mind there is only emptiness. There are no analytical categories we can apply to the experience, because our whole being is caught up in it. No part of us stands aside. We might imagine that a fish (if it had human intelligence) would find it hard to analyze the wetness of water because it has no experience of being dry. We are likewise immersed in God. The result may be little in the way of insights or information about God. It may seem as though we "know" less now than we did before; hence, the use of the words unknowing, emptiness, and darkness which point to our inability to conceptualize about God. Nevertheless, our relationship with God is deeper than when God was simply an object of our observation.

So the dark night of absence and emptiness is not just an experience of the loss of the previous modes by which the awareness of God's gifts had been mediated to us; it is a shift to a new way of knowing. This new way of knowing leaves our analytical faculties in darkness and gives an intellectual sense of absence just at the point of deepest relationship.

The second shift in knowing which occurs in this dark night is a change in the categories of knower and known. As we have seen, God is no longer an object to be known.

---

[2]Thomas Merton, "Philosophy of Solitude," *Disputed Questions*. New York: Farrar, Straus & Giroux, 1960, p. 189.

Just as significantly, we discover that we are not the primary knower. The primary knower is God. It is we who are known by and in God. The process of entering into a deep relationship with God is also the process of uncovering ourselves. Those places inside ourselves which we have hidden from the world, and even from our own consciousness, are now opened for God to reorder. Those deep hurts we had walled off for protection can finally be healed. The angers, fears, and lusts we had rationalized away are revealed for what they are. We can be transformed and healed by God's love. This can happen because we no longer must prove our essential worth to ourselves, hiding that which does not meet our approved self-image. Now we know ourselves as God knows us, as ones who are loved by God. In the light of that love, deep re-patterning can take place in us. Out of this experience of being known by God we can know others in the same way, as those who are loved by God.

Love is the most common word used by journeyers to describe the relationship with God found in this new way of knowing. God's love not only transforms us but holds us in close relationship through eternity. Our response, in return, can be only love. In the dark night, knowing and loving are one.

We recognize this unity in our human interaction as well. To love another is to know the other at a deeper level than simply knowing information about the other. The Bible uses the word "know" in this way. When Genesis says that Adam knew Eve, it is speaking both about the sexual act and the concomitant deep relationship of loving and knowing that existed between the two. It is not accidental that some mystics, especially those in the apophatic tradition, have used marital imagery and the language of love to

speak about their relationship with God and God's relationship with us.

We can understand something of the meaning of this
imagery in our ordinary human interactions. It need not
apply to physical intimacy alone. When I was ill after
surgery and not able to be up and around to meet the new
group of students who arrived at the beginning of my
school's winter term, my mother, who came to care for
me, would provide little descriptions of the newcomers. I
gathered quite a bit of information about the new students
in this manner and thought I knew them quite well. When
I finally went to class and met them in person, however,
my knowing of them changed so radically that I was taken
aback by how little my knowledge about them had any
bearing on my knowing of these people as friends. A very
different level of experience was opened in face-to-face
interaction, a much fuller and deeper knowing. It made
my knowledge about the people (their physical appear-
ances, professions, and places of origin) secondary.

The unity of knowing and loving in this new relationship
with God has implications for all areas of our lives. Usually
we see these two elements of human life, knowing and
loving, as very different and even opposed functions. If
they become separated from one another and their source
in God, however, they become demonic in quality. "Knowing about" is not a complete way of knowing. True knowing must be united in love. On the most fundamental level,
there is no way we can know without entering into loving
relationship with that which is known. Otherwise, knowing is merely an exploitation of the other. In contemporary
society, we see the danger of this way of knowing very
clearly. We know much about the earth, but cut off from
relationship with the earth, our knowledge simply leads

to despoiling the environment in our efforts to secure the earth's gifts. Modern education gives us a great deal of information about peoples around the globe. Without a sense of oneness with others, however, we use that information to jockey for military, economic, or political control over other people. In the dark night we learn from this new way of knowing that we must be willing to enter a relationship of commitment and fidelity if we wish to know the other as more than an object which is subject to our analysis. Moreover, as we move into the dark night mode of knowing we discover our oneness with other people and with the whole of creation is already given in and through God.

Just as knowing is transformed in the dark night, so loving is also transformed. Journeyers learn that love is not the sentimental stuff of popular tunes and valentine cards. Love is not chemical attraction or ego satisfaction. These latter kinds of "love" are not different from the possessive use of the other which too often characterizes our patterns of living. The way of unknowing (or deeper knowing) prevents our loving from becoming a narcissistic demand for our own fulfillment from the other (whether the other is another person, God, our "selves," or other elements in our natural world). In the dark night we undertake the painful restructuring process of learning how to love and be loved.

4

Contemplative Prayer:
Available to All

Deeper knowing (i.e., unknowing or loving) is what the Christian tradition has called contemplation. It is a way of prayer, but it might be better understood as a whole way of being. Too often we perceive prayer as a pious act: folded hands, closed eyes, and thoughtful words. True prayer may take place through these forms. Contemplation, however, has nothing to do with carrying out a pious act. Rather, it means entering into the kind of relationship with God which is characterized by unknowing.

The Christian heritage customarily defines contemplation in distinction to meditation as a style of prayer. Meditation is the systematic reflection on an idea, biblical verse, an image (e.g., the cross), or a question. Meditation involves using the mind to explore the religious implications of a chosen subject, i.e., how the subject brings us closer to God, what it reflects about our faithfulness or lack of faithfulness, what it enables us to learn about ourselves and our relationship with Christ, and so forth. Meditation is a powerful avenue of prayer.

Contemplation describes a different kind of prayer, the pure gift of being with God. In this prayer, systematic exploration of a theme becomes impossible. Even devotional reading seems useless. Many people who have had rich prayer lives may wonder what has happened to them, if such a dramatic change takes place. They are undergoing the shift in knowing which was described above. The analytical faculties which were used so richly in meditation are now silent. They can force no meaning or insights from what they read or think about. Because of the exterior stripping process, the old ways of experiencing God's gifts in the world have disappeared.

In this situation it may no longer be possible to "know about" God, but it is possible to enter a new and deeper relationship with God. In the darkness, contemplative prayer may begin.

Some religious literature portrays contemplation as the culmination of a life of prayer, an experience given only to an elite few who are spiritually advanced enough or psychically gifted enough to receive such a mystical awareness. Faithful preparation and discipline, both in prayer and in daily living, are most often the ground out of which a deeper relationship with God may grow. Careful watchers of the spiritual life, however, discern that contemplative prayer is not reserved only for a special few. It comes to many people. It can come at almost any time. We can "fall through" to this other way of knowing at any moment. It is not the result of our cumulative efforts to bring ourselves to a pinnacle of prayer.

In fact, contemplation is not an "experience" in the usual sense of the term. It may be closer to the truth to call it a non-experience, for its qualities are darkness, absence, and emptiness. (Remember, contemplation does not mean visions, voices, and lights.) These contemplative non-experiences come to us all. They may often come not when things are going well and we feel ourselves the masters and mistresses of our fate, but when our lives seem to be lying in pieces around us, when all that had carried meaning for us is broken. We struggle desperately to find a firm foundation on which we can build a new life. But at such times there may be no humanly constructed way to wholeness. Nothing that we can think about or envision or do will affect our situation in a positive way. We are left stripped of all that is significant with no place to turn.

One helpful interpretation of this predicament comes from a contemporary Carmelite, Sr. Constance FitzGerald.[1] The Carmelites have a rich heritage of interpretive writings on the dark night, a living legacy inspired by their sixteenth-century reformer, John of the Cross. Constance FitzGerald calls this predicament an "impasse experience." An impasse is a situation where there is no rational solution. All people encounter such circumstances from time to time: the marriage which appears dead; the job which no longer provides meaning; the unbearable burdens of school, peer expectations, and family pressures which make some young people think of suicide. Just at this failure of our rational and analytical thought processes to give us an answer, however, we are forced to a place of darkness and, thence, to a new way of knowing. What we perceive as darkness and emptiness appears to those familiar with the apophatic way as contemplation or the ground out of which contemplation may arise. When we are forced beyond the usual analytical levels of knowing because we have exhausted the possibilities found there, we move to unknowing. In this empty place, we may meet God.

Contemplative experience has been compared to right

---

[1] See her chapter "Impasse and Dark Night" in Tilden Edwards (ed.), *Living with Apocalypse: Spiritual Resources for Social Compassion*. San Francisco: Harper & Row, 1984, pp. 93-116.

brain activity, that part of our brain which is given to creative, insightful, integrative functions. This kind of thinking is distinguished from the very different analyzing work of the left brain. Current physiological studies cast doubt on whether the brain can be so neatly categorized into two parts with two separate functions assigned to each part. The two kinds of knowing still occur even if they cannot be assigned neatly to only one part of the brain.

Contemplative experience often results in creative restructuring of our patterns of thought and behavior. In the death of the old, the new can appear. Through being stripped of the usual inward ideas and illusions about ourselves, our world, and even about God, we are able to let go of narrow or false understandings of the nature of human existence which were manufactured out of our fears, hurts, angers, and desires or were passed along by the social order in which we live. As a result we are able to see more clearly. We are released from enslavement to false expectations and wrong desires. Our lives are now centered in that empty place with God. Out of that new centering comes a freedom to make new decisions, to see new truth, and to enter into a new pattern of life.

The way forward out of the impasse situation is not through the old pattern (which is now shattered anyway) but through a new pattern which emerges as a gift from God. Usually the new pattern is built around a level of meaning in our lives which we never knew was there. It may be the discovery of eternal life, along with the life we know in time. It may be an awareness that God is found in weakness and not just in strength. In each case the meaning and direction come as a gift out of the darkness and not as the result of our drive to build our own world of meaning.

Sr. Constance FitzGerald suggests that this contemplative process can and must be entered into by whole communities and nations, not just individuals. She does not mean that everyone must become a monk or spend hours in a chapel praying. She means that collectively we must recognize those places of impasse and enter the darkness and emptiness which face us.

Society today faces countless dilemmas about which there seems no rational solution, try as we might to find one. Our world-wide efforts to find peace while we plunge ever closer to war is a case in point. We mobilize peace groups, write letters to government officials, try to negotiate weapons-reduction agreements and to find peaceful ways of resolving international conflict. Progress is made in solving some problems, yet desperate conditions continue in many areas of the world. Conditions of political and economic injustice, the breeding ground of war, are more solidly entrenched around the world than ever. In many areas of conflict our efforts to bring justice have been useless and we are further from peace than we ever were. Constance FitzGerald recommends that we recognize when all these efforts have not brought a solution. It is likely in these situations that more of the same kind of effort will be no more successful than it has in the past. Something new must happen, but this can occur only if we allow ourselves to face the darkness and emptiness of the world we have created and the absence of resources to heal our own brokenness. In the stripping of our arrogance and pretensions which goes on in that dark place, we face a shattering of our old world. Perhaps for the first time we can also enter into a deep relationship with the One who can help us face our hidden blocks and fears, who can re-pattern our stifled and broken lives, and who can recon-

cile the seemingly irreconcilable. In the darkness the old
self will die; only then can we accept God's gift of resurrection.

5

Difficulties Along the Way

The dark night journey is sometimes a long one. It may extend over a number of months or even years, although in long periods of darkness there are commonly times of intermission when God graciously grants a sense of divine presence, direction, and reassurance. The intensity of the journey, then, is not always at the same level for all of this time.

The journey is a remarkably sure and safe one. Because the way is so dark and the transformation so deep, one might imagine that much could go wrong. This is rarely the case. In fact, many journeyers come to feel the darkness is their protection. Because we cannot see where else to turn, we have no choice but simply to allow God to continue the work. This saying yes to God is what allows the divine healing and transforming work to come to fruition.

There are some places, however, where we may encounter difficulties or find ourselves wishing to say no to God. These situations can block the movement of the journey and prevent us from living lives completely centered in God. Most often these difficulties grow out of the dilemmas of our own lives, but sometimes they arise because of the religious language used to talk about the spiritual life. Lest that happen here, it may be helpful to say a word about two of the metaphors which are commonly used in describing a time of darkness and stripping. These two metaphors are of the inward journey and the death of self.

Inward Journey

The metaphor of an inward journey is often used to speak of the transformational aspects of the dark night experience. The idea of a journey can be helpful or detrimental.

There are potential problems with journey imagery. Some people experience their relationship with God much more as dwelling at home rather than as pilgrimage or traveling. Indeed, dwelling with God is a profound image for the dark night. It gathers up much of our experience of "being" rather than "doing" while we are in the darkness. Moreover, the idea of a journey may inappropriately conjure up a sense of "progress" in the spiritual life; consequently, we tend to think we can hurry along in this "journey" or somehow bring ourselves out of the bewildering place of darkness through some effort of our own. To try by our effort to hurry may be especially tempting when thinking about the difficulties we may encounter in the darkness. Of course, the dark night is precisely the time in our lives when we recognize that we cannot force God, others, or even ourselves to "progress" anywhere. Our role is that of being willing to cooperate with God. It does no good to outrun our Guide.

On the other hand, there is a wonderful quality in the metaphor of a journey. This quality is very much needed when we may be caught up in pain, bewilderment, and despair. We need hope that God is at work, even though we may not be able to "see" or "feel" it. Most people do not experience a sense of dwelling with God when confronting the painful barriers which can exist in the dark night. It is very comforting to learn from others that they have drawn closer to God in the midst of what may seem an empty waste. The metaphor of the journey helps us know that this "drawing closer" is possible. We are not just left with the barriers and stumbling blocks. Hope gives us the courage to continue allowing God to lead us when we cannot see our way.

In discussing the difficulties we encounter in the dark night, let us use the image of the inward journey as a way to express our hope and trust in God, not as a way of "progressing" in the spiritual life. Let us also keep in mind that our home is in and with God.

Death of Self

Our understanding of our "self" changes radically during a time of darkness and stripping. Many people speak about this radical change as a death of self. While this image is very apt in one way, it can also be misleading. The term death of self does not mean the extinguishing of our personhood. Rather it speaks of the extinguishing of our previous way of defining and experiencing ourselves in the world

We all experience changes in self-perception as we go through life. We are constantly growing and maturing. The self-understanding we had as a small child is not the same as we have as an adult. This maturation can and does go on in periods of spiritual darkness and emptiness. This change in self-perception is one small part of what is meant by the imagery of the death of self.

There is, however, a much deeper change that is taking place during this time than a movement toward greater psychological maturity. The dark night is not a stage of growth that can be placed on a graph that charts ego-development. It does not precede or follow any particular "level" of maturity. This experience can come to anyone, at any age, at any stage of psychological growth, or with any self-understanding.

In the usual course of events we define ourselves by our talents, skills, weaknesses, and shortcomings. We perceive this "self" as managing, planning, and arranging our lives and all the events, people, and problems that come our way. We measure our worth by how well this management takes place. During the course of our lives, important inward transformations may take place on this level of awareness. For example, we may come to recognize that a sense of low esteem has blocked us from recognizing the talents we do have. We may not have been able to respond faithfully to God as a result. Our changed understanding may now make it possible to live life more faithfully and fully.

In the darkness, however, there is a movement away from autonomous images of ourselves, whatever the content of those images, toward a deeper, more relational sense of personhood. We become aware that ultimately we cannot be defined by our strengths and weaknesses. We exist because God creates and sustains us. We live in and through God. This deeper awareness comes in the gift of contemplative prayer. In the dark night this awareness also comes in the experience of daily living, as we move away from our autonomous understanding of self to a recognition that we live in and through God. This deeper self cannot be measured, analyzed, or defined. Its worth does not depend on its talents and skills. It cannot even be perceived as an object. We are grounded in God. We can only live into the reality of our relationship from the inside, so to speak. We cannot measure it from the outside. Clinging to our analytical image of ourselves can block this deeper awareness. The image of the death of self refers to the movement from the perception of ourselves as an object to that of living and being in relationship with God. Language about the death of self does not reflect a masochistic desire to denigrate who we are. It is an experiential way of speaking about the letting go of our analytical self-defining to accept our life as given in and through God. Many writers speak about the death of the autonomous image of ourselves as the death of the false self. Living into the reality of our life in God is called the birth of the true self.

This deeper awareness may have a profound effect on our behavior and even on our analytical perception of ourselves. The dark night does not extinguish all the traits and characteristics which make us the particular persons we are. These traits grow out of our genetic structure, our personal and social histories, the ongoing circumstances of our lives, and the choices we make in the midst of these givens. Some of our traits are easily changeable; some may be changed only with great effort; some probably cannot be changed at all in the ordinary course of human events. But our centeredness in God now allows us to see ourselves and our problems differently. We may be able, for example, to let go of our sense of worthlessness or the need to cling defensively to that which makes us feel worthy. We now know worth does not come from a scorecard which measures our gifts.

For many people this movement from perception of ourselves as autonomous objects to centeredness in God moves relatively smoothly. For others there can be problems. It is worthwhile to mention several of the most common difficulties. Very often just being able to perceive the difficulty and the reason it is blocking the path is enough to allow us to continue the journey.

The difficulties that block movement in the dark night usually come from the interior responses of the journeyer. Three "blocking" responses common to people in different parts of the dark night journey are anger, terror, and distorted selflessness. Each is an understandable human reaction to the severe stripping which may be encountered along the way. It is natural to focus on that which has been taken away, yet each response can become destructive if it causes the journeyer to focus on self rather than God.

Anger

Anger is a widespread response to the outward losses which may be part of the dark night and which, in turn, occasion the more general experience of loss of meaning, direction, and divine presence. In fact, it would be unusual to go through a dark night period without anger at all.

Anger may increase as the journey into darkness progresses, because the parts of our environment which we can control are drastically reduced. Countless circumstances may curtail our outward lives. Inwardly, prayer is no longer ours to direct. We discover our own finitude. When that part of ourselves which manipulates, arranges, and plans has no materials with which to work, the structure of the old self-understanding begins to crack open. Then the deeper self can emerge.

We are like a seed whose hard husk is beginning to break when it is planted in the dark, wet earth. From the dissolution of that seed comes the tender new plant. Since we are human beings, not seeds, we often react to this process by trying to cling to whatever vestiges of control we have. We fear our inability to control ourselves and our environment. Without such control we feel helpless. Our response to this fear and helplessness is anger. Anger is, then, among the last strongholds of the old, false self. As the journey continues, even our anger must be stripped away as we suffer the crucifixion of our narrow self-will and move from anger to love.

This description of the movement through anger to love is not meant to be a call to suppress our natural reaction to circumstances of human injustice or to terrible situations of human suffering. We may have experienced sexual abuse as a child. We may find our professional advancement blocked as the result of racial prejudice. We may have lost a loved one through an accident, illness, or even homicide. These horrendous situations cannot be wished away. Anger makes us aware of the depth of real problems which confront us. Sometimes the situations can be rectified. We can answer the call to work toward justice and healing. Some situations are not so easily in our control. We are left to confront the pain of uncontrollable circumstances. In either case anger is a reaction that can point toward the desire for wholeness, justice, and healing. Those people who hide from their anger or bury it out of reach deep within themselves need help to get back in touch with this basic emotion. Ultimately, however, anger must give way to deeper understanding or we find that we stumble over ourselves in our very movement toward that wholeness.

If the initial response of anger does not give way before God's gift of love, a journeyer may develop one of two chronic attitudes which may be very destructive. The first attitude is bitterness, a chronic pattern of resentment where the anger is directed outwardly toward other people or toward God. With this attitude we see others as the primary cause of our dilemma and pain; indeed, other people may have committed great wrongs. Anger is our way of striking back at them. But ongoing bitterness paralyzes us in our move toward a deeper wholeness. A second chronic attitude is that of despair, an inward focusing of the same feelings of anger. This causes emotional withdrawal, apathy, or depression. When we withdraw into apathy, we build a wall around us to protect ourselves from the real world and the pain of living there. Both reactions bypass the one thing which makes us able to deal with our pain and the problems of unfairness and injustice which we may confront in the world around us—God's love.

The fulfillment of our journey toward God is found in this love. One key that may help us move beyond anger to love is to see the journey from God's perspective, so to speak, rather than from our own sense of loss. This does not mean that God ultimately causes or sanctions our loss for the sake of some "spiritual good." But God can and does work in the midst of our loss and pain to help us enter more deeply into the divine life and become part of God's redemptive work in the world. For this to occur we must die to our former, constricted experience of self and be ready to enter God's new life of love. This is the meaning of our participation in Christ's crucifixion and resurrection.

This movement from anger to love is not a process in which we are passive bystanders. Very often we look at anger, bitterness, and despair as psychological forces over which we have no control. That is not entirely true. They are powerful emotions which, if not worked through, tend to block our ability to see how God is at work in our midst. But we have the choice of saying yes or no to these emotions. They can hinder us from taking the next step in our spiritual lives which is to say yes to God's gift of love. But they cannot destroy completely our power to choose. We can take steps to work through our emotions and to say yes to God. In fact, we must say yes for that love to take root and grow. God will not impose even love upon us. In practice we may need to say yes again and again to avoid being swept up in the former destructive, angry patterns. But having said yes to God's love, that love will ultimately have the power to cast out our anger, bitterness, and despair.

As we accept God's love in the midst of our pain, brokenness, and unfaithfulness, we can hear Christ's promises of reconciliation, healing, and forgiveness to us. Thus, we can help convey them to our broken world. Having known anger and loss, we can be one with those who also know this pain. We have become one both with those who inflict their anger on others and those who are victims of other people's pain. We are one with all those who feel blocked from God's presence. To those who feel no hope we can bring the promise of love. Christians know this love historically in the life and death of Jesus. In the dark night we discover this Christ-love continuing to be poured out on us. By participating in Christ's crucifixion we are enabled to become one with his love which reaches out to all who are in pain, anger, or brokenness: the poor, the ill in mind and body, the forgotten ones. In the dark night we learn to love and become participants in Christ's redemptive work today.

Terror

One of the most painful experiences people encounter in the dark night is that movement toward death of the old understanding of self. Most of us are aware that this movement is taking place. There is usually a part of us which is willing to cooperate with this movement and looks forward to the new life which God will bring forth. But there is always a part of each of us which fears to let go of the old way and resists the birth of the new.

In the crucifixion of the dark night, death may be experienced on several levels. We can usually recognize daily life activities which block us. A loved one is dead and not there to share the joys and pains of everyday living. Illness may threaten the continuation of life. Divorce or loss of a job may take away the main source of purpose, direction, and fulfillment. The death which a person confronts in the dark night, however, is not only the loss of one or more significant elements of life. It is not necessarily even a confrontation with physical death, although this may be part of the reality we face. This crucifixion is a reorganization of personhood. We are not only called to make adjustments to one or more traumatic situations but to move into a whole new way of being. For the new structure of person-hood to appear, the old structure must die. Sometimes we even live out the confrontation with death on a symbolic level through dreams or waking visions.

Occasionally observers interpret dreams and visions as signs of neurotic tendencies coming to the fore. This analysis is not very helpful. More useful is to recognize that our minds and bodies are so made that symbols and inward images work within us, even in the dark night journey. The intensity of the journey may just make us more aware of the process.

I have met deeply religious, highly gifted, and very sensitive people who feared, in the midst of their dark night journeys, that they would burn up through sponta-neous combustion, be destroyed by mechanical monsters, or be shot. Each person was quite clear that these scenarios were taking place within their own minds, but the reality of these symbols created sheer terror for each person. All feared physical death. All wondered if they should allow themselves to die. They felt they might be thwarting the call to death if they did not physically die and thus allow the process to go to completion. Each of the people who experienced a symbolic confrontation with death had to find a symbolic experience of new life in order to enter fully into his or her new way of being in actual, daily living. In their prayers, dreams, or in daily living they confronted that which symbolized death for them. Each discovered a new, more joyous and integrated life on the other side of the experience.

Very often our fears prevent us from entering the new life that God is offering to us. We need to recognize that God leads us through this experience of death and rebirth not out of disregard for our welfare, but just the opposite.

God is trying to bring us into close relationship, but that is not possible unless we let go of the former understanding of self. Our fear comes because we see only from the perspective of the dying self, not God's perspective which sees what will be born. If we can turn our focus from self to God, the fear will be gone. Of course, when we turn attention from self to God the transformation is accomplished.

We may find it helpful to remember consciously all those occasions where God has been present as a help in times of trouble. We can remember that Christ has gone before us and has overcome death. These memories may allow us to go forward on faith from past experience, even though the end of the journey cannot be seen at this juncture.

Self and Selflessness

A third potential difficulty in the dark night may occur toward the end of the journey. This is the problem of passivity and of a distorted sense of selflessness.

The journeyer knows well by this time that the call is away from control by the autonomous self, toward centeredness in God. The individual recognizes how self-centered (in the spiritual sense, not necessarily in a moral sense) his or her life has been and now tries to cooperate with God by giving up self-will.

Two problems may occur at this point. The first is that journeyers may become unduly focused on their own sinfulness. We can be overwhelmed by the realization of all

the ways we have said no to God and clung to our autonomous image of self. Separation from God becomes the
center of our perception rather than God's promise of
reconciliation. The answer, of course, is to focus on God
rather than on self or on sinfulness. Clinging to the focus
on sinfulness is, paradoxically, a way of clinging to the
focus on self.

The second problem is that journeyers may have a mistaken notion that giving up self-will means having no
initiative, preferences, likes, and needs. They become almost invisible in the environment. They are afraid to express a preference lest that be a sign of following self-will
rather than God's will; they will not speak an opinion for
fear this is coercion of others.

Great sensitivity in this matter is in order, for it is a sign
of growing awareness of the centeredness on self that brings
this carefulness. These very scrupulous reactions may be
good and helpful discipline and training to reestablish a
rightful balance. This is especially true in contemporary
North American society which places so much emphasis
on self-fulfillment and self-expression, both perceived in
very individualistic ways. Our society does not provide us
with very reliable criteria or standards by which to judge
our Christian self-understanding. The dark night brings a
strong prophetic critique of some of the shallow understandings of selfhood espoused in our culture.

Beyond this reestablishing of a rightful understanding
and expression of self, the outward circumstances of the
dark night journey often militate against much self-directed
activity at this time. It is not that the person makes a
decision not to act or to speak, but that circumstances do
not allow such choices. Living through this experience
permits the full reorientation of self, permits the shift in

awareness from life arising out of oneself to life arising from God.

In general, it is safest not to encourage more expression of self at this time than the person feels inwardly is faithful to God's call. This means both the journeyer and the nurturer must remain very close to the movement of the Spirit in the life of the journeyer to discern what is right. This prescription is necessary because in our activist culture it is very easy to jump to the conclusion that something is wrong with the extended period of quiet and listening which so often characterizes a person who is drawn along an apophatic path.

There are exceptions, however, to the general rule of trusting a quiet, listening role. These exceptions apply to journeyers who have moved very far in their transformation toward centeredness in God, yet somewhere along the way have forgotten that a separate self exists or have so ignored the legitimate expression of personhood that they need encouragement to blossom forth fully. These journeyers may need help remembering that our movement toward God is an indication that we are real. The point of this journey is not to disappear but to be centered in God. The result of the journey is to receive the gift of oneself, one's real self. If the journey is followed to its end, we will discover a healthy sense of self, now rooted in God. We will not be left with a thwarted sense of unfulfillment. Some journeyers may need special encouragement to recognize and accept the gift of personhood rooted in God.

The language of "surrender to God," used so commonly among those who have found themselves in darkness, can create difficulties for some people. The call to surrender does not refer to surface relinquishing of one's desires, wishes, and thoughts. Indeed, such a superficial meaning of surrender can be dangerous. Rightly used, surrender means faithfulness. It means saying yes to God's call to be the person God created us to be. There are occasions when surrender to God may call for letting go of our protective, clinging behavior on one or more levels; surrender, however, may also incorporate a very active and determined stance in daily life to own who we are on the deepest level. Surrender may, in addition, involve a strong critique of the existing social order.

This problem in language is exacerbated by unfortunate developments in some strands of Christian spirituality which portray Christian life as a doormat kind of existence: love of God and love of others means no regard for self. To have any feelings, criticisms, preferences, opinions, or sense of self-worth is seen as selfish. Of course, just the opposite is true. We cannot love others or God unless we are full persons. We cannot live God's new order unless we are able to stand against the unrighteousness in our world. These denigrating attitudes have been especially crippling for a great many women in our society. They have also affected many men. As a result many people have a pervasive sense of worthlessness. Even more damaging is the theological misperception that God wishes us to dislike and punish ourselves. We need to reclaim the fullness of the Christian faith. God creates us in love to be full, vibrant human beings. Much of God's work in the world happens through the fullness of our deepest love and concern for one another and for ourselves.

A sense of inferiority or worthlessness is one of the most pervasive experiences of contemporary people. Feelings of superiority and inferiority are both reflections of self-centeredness. Very often Christian teaching has concentrated on the dangers of pride or our more subtle "need" to control and direct the world around us. These are real dangers in our relationship with God and with others. The dark night powerfully strips away a false sense of self-sufficiency. In a paradoxical way, it also addresses the seemingly opposite, but really identical, problem of a sense of inadequacy and non-worth. The problem is identical because in both cases the person is "measuring" the worth of a supposedly autonomous self. The solution to the sense of inadequacy is not to give the ego a boost, although it may be helpful to give the person a more accurate reality-check if she cannot see her place in the world clearly. The deeper answer is to stop using the measuring rod which assumes that our self-worth is rooted in our achievement. This can happen by directing the focus of one's life to God and away from self (whether we feel inadequate or super-adequate about ourselves or whether we experience the common human malady of swinging back and forth between these two views). When God is the center and we see ourselves as a gift of God, then the feelings of inadequacy or superiority can die away. Our personhood is not something which must be proved by some external standard or by a competitive exam. It does not depend on our brilliance or beauty or sparkling personality. Our worth comes from the reality that God creates, loves, and sustains us. Our contribution is living fully and faithfully as the person God creates, loves, and sustains. Through being that person we become a witness and pointer to God.

Journeyers in the dark night need to claim the fullness of their own personhood. For some journeyers the stripping consists in giving up feelings of inadequacy. Strangely, this may be as frightening as any other form of stripping, because it is the same radical attack on self-centeredness that is rooted in our old sense of autonomous self. As with other forms of stripping away of false supports, it is also a liberation that allows us to enter God's new order.

6

Three Special Occasions
of the Dark Night Journey

There are three special occasions in human life when the dark night journey is particularly apt to be our primary spiritual path: the extreme curtailment of human activity, facing death, and inward preparation for ministry and mature Christian living.

Extreme Curtailment of Human Activity and Independent Living

The dark night understandings are of utmost importance for those people who face extreme curtailment of human activity as an ongoing way of life. Those who are imprisoned for long periods, those who have been born with extreme congenital problems, and those who contract a severe, debilitating sickness are often ill-served by the discussions of Christian life and spirituality which are predominant in contemporary society. Most of the spirituality coming from the *via moderna* mode of spiritual understanding emphasizes involvement with others, active service, work to change and correct the problems of this world. God is perceived primarily through work in the midst of

this world. While there is much that is good in this emphasis, it leaves us with little to say to the persons who,
by force of circumstance, can never participate in this form
of spirituality. What relevance does the Christian faith have
for them? How do they perceive that their lives have
meaning?

We begin to see the effects of this one-sided spirituality
in many ways. In the news there is a report of a bright,
personable young woman in her twenties with cerebral
palsy. She wishes to end her life because it is so restricted
she feels it is not worth living. A family with a severely
retarded newborn wishes to leave the infant unfed, because
if it were to grow up it could not live a "full" life, a life
of quality. A grandmother in her nineties also decides that
it is better to stop eating and to die than to place the burden
on her family of having to care for her now that her frailty
requires that she be dependent on others. A young man,
active in the social justice movement in his country, is
imprisoned by a repressive government. He now feels his
existence is pointless because his life had meaning only
through his active political work. We measure life so completely by productivity, accomplishment, independence,
and participation in the ordinary activities of mainstream
society that we can see no reason for life if we are cut off
from these things.

Those involved in religious teaching and spiritual nurture must ask themselves serious questions about how
much the contemporary church has been seduced by the
culture around it. In an effort to make our spirituality
relevant, it may simply have become a reflection of, at
worst, a shallow set of secular values or, at best, a one-sided
perception of the meaning of life and our relationship with
God. The apophatic categories of the dark night journey

bring a prophetic critique to contemporary social and religious values which see life as worth living only if it meets the mark of success in terms of productivity, activity, and independence. The apophatic path perceives meaning when virtually all outward avenues of involvement in this world are closed to us. It is precisely then that we can see that life has as its goal the relationship with God. This relationship can grow even stronger just when it seems there is nothing outwardly to give life meaning. This relationship does not depend even on our immediate experiential sense of God's presence. A life lived in trust and dependence on God is a radical witness to the Eternal One who does not measure out love based on an external standard of worth. All meaning ultimately rests in that love which extends beyond time.

Facing Death

One of the most difficult situations in life is that of facing our own death or the death of a loved one. The frailty of advanced age, diagnosis of terminal illness, or life-threatening persecution can bring us to the awareness of our own mortality and finitude. We realize that nothing in this world can be our ultimate support. We may face only darkness and emptiness. This awareness may be part of a dark time of stripping of all that is finite. In death we yield our final "possession," our physical bodies. With that ultimate surrender comes the possibility of entering into a new way of knowing God.

Of course, not all people who face death, illness, or other

extreme situations go through a dark night. Not all face the loss of God's presence. In fact, they may be granted the experience of God's close presence and comfort. Such people may learn much during this time of pain and suffering, but they do not necessarily enter the contemplative way of knowing or undergo the particular kind of re-patterning associated with the dark night path. In short, God does not use all such situations to take people through a dark night journey. There are many pathways in which we come to close relationship with God. It is, therefore, inappropriate to assume that all who face these situations will find the explorations of the apophatic way helpful. They should never be imposed.

While not all who face death journey in a dark night, a number will find they are led this way. Because the apophatic tradition faces loss and emptiness squarely, it is in a unique position to speak to those who find themselves in this place. In the popular mind the dark night pathway is terrifying and pitiless. Those who are not on such a journey themselves may find its description discomforting, but for those who are in the midst of the journey, the reactions are usually very different. They feel a breath of hope to know that other people have come this way before them and have left some guideposts to help them on their way. For the first time they may recognize that they are on a journey which has a goal: a deep relationship with God which exists above and beyond the finite modes of expression in this world and in this life.

Much contemporary work with people in severe distress is geared to removing the distress. Certain models of medical and psychological help have this aim. It is appropriate for these fields. Whatever help and alleviation they can bring to people in pain is a godsend, yet this very mind-set, i.e., removal of pain and distress, may make the situation worse for some people. Our whole society is oriented to success, achievement, wholeness, and wellness. We feel there is a way to fix all problems. The pain of death, debilitating illness, and the growing frailty of advanced age are put in an impossible category. We look for rescue and feel betrayed if we cannot find it.

The apophatic tradition does not try to rescue a person from the darkness, but rather looks for a way to live in the darkness with trust. It believes God is there in our brokenness and emptiness. In the apophatic tradition our attention turns toward God and not toward escaping the emptiness. During those times in our lives when there is no way out, no solution to a problem, when death is inevitable, the gleanings from the dark night journey may be more helpful than any other aid. They bring us face to face with the other-worldly or eternal dimension of our Christian faith. We discover a new way of knowing and loving God which transcends the categories of this world.

It is important to realize that the journey may not come to its fruition in this life. Death may cut short the fullness of the new way of knowing God. One danger in describing this journey and its importance for our deepening relationship with God is that we may begin to treat it as though it were a process under our control, a spiritual technique we can tuck away as part of our mastery of the mysteries of life. While, by the grace of God, we can see some things about this journey as we and others embark upon it, this journey, above all others, is not under our control. It is not we, who by dint of our skill or prayer, uncover any deeper insights about our relationship with God. There is no way we can take ourselves or others out of the dark night. Nor can we take ourselves or others to the end of the journey, that place of transformation and new relationship with God. These are gifts from God alone. Our experience may be only the pain, the loss, and the increasing sense of distance from God. Both journeyers and nurturers must be prepared to face the reality that the dark night may get darker as the person moves farther in the journey. Both can only continue in the faith that this crucifixion will not be the end, but that God will bring resurrection and new life. The fullness of the journey may not be accomplished on this side of the grave. But Christ's crucifixion and resurrection give proof that death is not the end. We can trust that God is with us in death even though we see only darkness. Christ has gone before us and shown us that God's gift of new life awaits us.

Relationship of the Dark Night to Depression and Bereavement

Spiritual nurturers who work with people facing death frequently ask questions about the relationship of the dark night journey to depression and the grief process in bereavement. A word about each is in order.

The medical, psychological, and spiritual dimensions of the dark night and clinical depression may be very different. Depression, though, may be one element in a dark night journey. After distinguishing the two conditions (an important first step), one may find that any given individual is in the midst of both.

One helpful way to distinguish the two situations is to see whether the person is undergoing the re-patterning typical of the dark night. Is the person moving from centeredness on self to centeredness on God, with a deepening capacity to care for others? Is the person shifting into a contemplative way of knowing God? Does the person face an impasse situation or is the person too withdrawn to explore the available solutions to the problems of living? (The latter is characteristic of depression, which may be a protective block to ameliorate the pain of a deep hurt. While protecting the person from pain, depression may also make a full and free response to life impossible.) Finally, is the person able to carry on normal job requirements, interactions with family, friends, etc.? (In the dark night, the person is usually able to continue these functions.)

In cases of suspected depression, it may be helpful to find out if the experiences of darkness and sadness are cyclical. Are they related to identifiable hormonal imbalances (or deficiencies) or manic-depressive mood swings? (Both of these medical conditions can receive significant help today from new medications.) Also, is there evidence of buried anger or resentment which is blocking an affective and affirmative response to life? (A psychological counselor may be able to be of special help in these situations.) Of course, it is always important to be watchful for suicidal thoughts or behavior. If any of these situations prevail, one should seek further skilled medical or psychological help.

Ultimately, one must remember that depressions with medical and psychological causes and treatments may also be part of a larger dark night journey. No person lives in compartments with medical, psychological, and spiritual parts of themselves separated from the whole. One should take care not to use these definitions in a way that would cut off recognition of the psychological dimension of the dark night or the spiritual dimension of depression.

Very similar remarks may be made about the relationship between the dark night and bereavement. The dark night is a time of loss. Living with and through grief is a significant element in situations of loss, including the dark night; therefore, a knowledge of the grieving process may be helpful to spiritual nurturers who work with those on dark night journeys.

But the dark night is not just a synonym for grief. For in the dark night the primary focus is not on the loss. It is on the contemplative way of knowing God and on the re-patterning of life which comes from this contemplative form of knowing. Many people who encounter losses find that they are drawn to contemplation and deep re-patterning. But others do not experience their losses in this way. For them God will reveal different truths.

Moreover, the dark night does not necessarily entail any outward loss. The major component of the journey is the loss of the "experience" of God. Thus, while bereavement and the dark night may intertwine in some people's lives, they do not always do so. One should take care not to regard the two situations as identical.

Preparation for Ministry

Dark night journeys are not restricted to those who are going through severe or life-threatening outward situations. God may lead us through this pathway at any point in life. Such journeys often come to those whom God is bringing to greater maturity in Christian life and preparing for deeper ministry.

Throughout our lives, God is at work in the outward circumstances of our living and through the interior movement of the Spirit. God is constantly drawing us into a deeper relationship, teaching us to receive and give love, and bringing us to the wholeness which, in our brokenness, we cannot create ourselves. All of this divine work is part of preparation for ministry (here understood as the call to servanthood sent to all Christians, not just those who are ordained ministers). In addition, however, many people experience a particular interior preparation that comes after an initial conversion. This often happens after they have made a serious commitment to Christ and dedicated themselves to God's service.

At this point God seems to get serious with us. However much we may think we have dedicated ourselves to God, we have, in fact, only begun the journey that ends in dedication. The initial commitment to God is usually an intellectual and emotional breakthrough. While the goals and activities in our lives may shift, the structure of our lives may remain the same. For example, we may, as the result of our initial movement toward God, give our time and effort to work in our church or help to meet the pressing social needs of our society. This shift in activity from our previous occupation or work to a more "religious" one may only be the beginning of the movement necessary for us. (Of course, our definition of "religious" may be too limited. Dedication to God can be manifested in myriad jobs.) The definition of "religious work" aside, it is all too easy to do the work of God in the same way as we have done all previous work. We undertake the work expecting our efforts to bring change. We measure ourselves (and others) by the level of involvement in this good work. We pride ourselves on now doing "the Lord's work." In

all of this there may be little change in the "self" orientation
of our work. The work is still ours. We are still the center
of it. Our life has not shifted so that God is the center at
all. Our direction and fulfillment are still rooted in our
sense of our own accomplishment and our own power.

At this point the radical stripping of the dark night may
begin. We are called to radical dependence on God. All the
outward props which we have associated with our progress
in the religious life are pulled away. We enter the dark night.
Outwardly we may lose our former avenue of service
through illness, opposition, or some other cause. Inwardly
the experiential sense of God's presence and direction re-
cedes. It looks as though our hope for a life committed to
God's service has disappeared. When we are left in poverty
and emptiness, without any finite thing to rely on, the true
meaning of that hope can be realized. Our life is finally in
God's hands, not our own. God leaves us in that condition
long enough for a deep interior restructuring of our being
to take place.

Two fundamental things happen. 1) We come to know
God in a more profound way than before. 2) The boulders in
our pathway, produced by ego-centeredness, are crumbled
to dust so that in our future ministry we will not stumble
over ourselves. Too often ministry fails at just this point.
There is so much self-will connected with it that we block
the movement of God in our very efforts to be a channel
for God's transforming love. For example, we are proud
of our skillful pastoral counseling. We are pleased with our
acumen in affecting change in the local government's attitude toward a toxic-waste site. We are busy speaking to
various citizen's groups about the dangers of nuclear war;
surely we will be rewarded for our efforts with the good
will of all who hear us. The measure of self-will still in us

is found in our anger with those who do not agree with our program. The re-patterning in our lives which can move us out of this framework in order to be truly centered on God is a massive one.

This re-patterning must be powerful enough to shake loose those deeply embedded impediments to a life centered in God. Then we can go forward in ministry without stumbling over major blocks coming from the old self-centered structure.

For those led in this path, the dark night journey is often the critical formation experience of their lives. This inward formation is more important than the outward training in ministry. It is unfortunate that much formal training in ministry does not even recognize that this inward preparation exists. In our world of degrees, exams, and training programs, it is easy to forget that ministry is not primarily a task; it is a way of being in the world. It is living in relationship with God and being a witness to God. Ministry is being able to listen to the Word of God and thereby have a word of life to share with others. Fundamentally, we do not *do* ministry. We *are* ministers. The experience of inward preparation for ministry is a confirmation of this reality.

We must recognize that God is the primary preparer for ministry. Our role is to recognize and cooperate with God's preparation work. Churches need tender and perceptive nurturers who can be of help to people whom God leads in this path of inward preparation.

Some Christian communities, past and present, have realized the prevalence and necessity of this inward pattern of spiritual formation and have tried to establish corporate structures of formation to aid in this process. Monastic communities through the centuries have had novitiate programs. At their best these programs anticipated, encouraged, and gave structural support to God's work of re-patterning going on in their new members. Some communities in the Protestant tradition have made similar corporate attempts to recognize the depth of interior transformation that goes on in the lives of members when they make a mature commitment to follow Christ. One historical example is the Methodist Church's use of the class meeting. More recently, some churches have experimented with small-group spiritual nurture programs of various kinds. These structures provide occasions to talk about faithful living and our deepening relationship with Christ.

Admittedly a formalized program can sometimes be just that, an external program unrelated to the actual work of God in a person's life. Even when there is no formal church recognition of the journey, the continued existence of the unplanned, inward dark night preparation in the lives of people from virtually every heritage suggests a need to look more carefully at ways to give nurture, support, and guidance to those whom God is calling to a deeper commitment and service.

Without support from one's church or meeting community, this dark night preparation for ministry can be fraught with special difficulties. Indeed, many who are led on this path of deeper preparation and surrender to God are paradoxically lost to the church and consequently to ministry. This phenomenon is so prevalent that many spiritual nurturers today perceive it as a critical problem in many religious communities.

The reason that certain dark night journeyers may be lost to their communities is two-fold. The first is the nature of the stripping that goes on for the journeyer in the inward preparation period. This may include the painful loss of an idealized vision of the church. The second is the failure of the church to recognize this specific dilemma or to offer any help meeting the difficulties encountered along the way. These people then struggle alone, experiencing increasing alienation from the community around them.

A little elaboration may make this problem clearer. As we have seen, the stripping process that goes on in any dark night makes us confront whatever element in our lives has taken the place of God. For most people that stripping confronts a hidden reliance on self. For those who are undergoing the inward preparation for ministry, the most painful loss may be that of the church itself. Of course, on a fundamental level, the church is a gift of God. The church does not stand on its own strength. In everyday living, however, it is easy to forget that reality. The church can become the ultimate embodiment of one's understanding of God's love and work in the world. For the dark night journeyers being led to ministry, helping the church become a more faithful body of Christ in the world is a central part of their commitment.

When these highly dedicated people are confronted with the potential for profound human frailties within the church, they may discover that the church-community is unfaithful in certain ways. It may be floundering in a sea of confusion. Perhaps the call to relevance has become a guise for adopting the values of the world. Busyness in programs of all kinds may be a way to hide from complete surrender to God, the kind of surrender that would make real changes in life necessary. To make matters worse most people in the church would just as soon not hear anything about its failures.

For those whose whole lives are dedicated to the church, this situation brings the collapse of their final pillar of support and plunges them into the dark night of emptiness.

It is no longer possible for them to see how God is working in our world, when even the church has no semblance of faithfulness. The church is not interested in their ministry; there is only darkness and absence.

Not surprisingly, John of the Cross, who has become recognized as the classic writer on the dark night, had to face a lax Carmelite tradition in sixteenth-century Spain. His own efforts at reform brought anger and persecution from within his own community. His life story is the experience of the collapse of this final human pillar of support.

From the point of view of God's preparation of us, our inappropriate use of this final human support must cease. Only then are we able to accept our radical dependence on God alone. All else is stripped away. Our human vision of the church and religious life must be dashed to pieces, not because it is wrong, but because it has become a barrier to our total surrender to God. We must learn how God would have us minister, not how we would like to minister. We must be able to function in the real world, not the world of idealistic dreams. We must be able to speak to people in the midst of their failures and brokenness and not be paralyzed by a sense of anger at these people for not living up to our visions. Only then is real participation in the church-community possible. Only then are we liberated to enter God's ministry.

Today many of the most sensitive and perceptive Christians are caught in feelings of hurt, betrayal, and despair over the loss of their idealistic image of the church. They withdraw from participation in the church-community. They give up the call to servanthood or ministry. Precisely because the church can be unperceiving or unfaithful, it offers little help to these most caring members. Paradoxically, these people are the ones needed to lead the church in this era, yet they are the ones we often ignore and turn away. We do not know how to deal with their hurt. Their prophetic vision is too uncomfortable in our lives.

Church leaders and spiritual nurturers must begin to be aware of the dark night preparation for ministry and the crisis of faith which it may entail for many people. Journeyers need support and understanding. Church-communities need to find ways of recognizing and appreciating the sometimes discomforting witness of those who have been stripped of all their idols and can see more clearly the idols belonging to the rest of us.

7

Ministry Growing
Out of the Dark Night

Those who travel in the dark night die to their old lives and are given new life in Christ. As the result of God's intensive work, journeyers live in a new relationship with God, self, and others. A significant number of these journeyers understand this time as an inward preparation for ministry. The ministry which flows from this pathway may manifest specific gifts in terms of content, but more importantly, it may bring a new way of being and living in the world, a way that can point others to God.

God-consciousness

The most prominent characteristic of the person who has been led through the dark night is a deep awareness of God. The person has become God-conscious. This consciousness pervades all of living. It does not necessarily mean that such people will have much to say about God nor even that they will use typical religious language. They have made a shift in orientation which is deeper than talking about God. This reality is present in the midst of all other concerns and activities. Hence, these persons often become witnesses to God through their very presence.

Oneness With Christ

A second aspect of this centeredness in God is a deepening awareness of oneness with Christ. This is a mystical awareness that reaches to the root of our everyday living. The experience of the death of the old self becomes one with Christ's crucifixion. The experience of new life is the experience of Christ's resurrection. Through the self-emptying experience of the dark night, the journeyer comes to understand the meaning of Christ's self-emptying at the incarnation: "Have this mind among yourselves, which you have in Christ Jesus, who, though he was in the form of God, did not count equality with God a thing to be grasped, but emptied himself, taking the form of a servant" (Philippians 2:5-7).

Christ gave himself fully to be with us in our pain and brokenness. His suffering was the result of full identification with the world's brokenness and pain. In the dark night, with Christ, the journeyer enters the experience of the world's brokenness and experiences the redemptive love of Christ.

This symbolic and mystical language of the Christian tradition, which before may have seemed only abstract doctrine, now is alive with meaning. It conveys an important quality of ministry as well. One does not simply come to the "end" of the dark night and then begin to minister. Rather ministry (servanthood) flows from our experience of ongoing oneness with Christ's self-emptying love. In the darkness we enter the suffering places in our world and in ourselves and know that God's love is there. The dark night, which on the one hand strips us of our idolatrous attachment to the things of this world, also brings us to deeper unity with all of God's creation.

Interior Freedom, Availability, Compassion

When discussing the ministry that arises out of the dark night time of self-emptying, many people speak not about what they do, but about the inner attitudes of heart and mind that allow them to do it. Above all, they describe being inwardly freed to be in relationship with God, with themselves, and with other people. This inward freedom is experienced in many ways. For some it is the freedom from dread. They have touched the depths of the world's pain and know that God's love is there. For others it is the ability to let go of compulsive or protective behavior. Because they have touched a deeper grounding in their lives, they no longer need to "prove" to themselves and others their own worth. Paradoxically, now that they are freed from having to prove how caring, loving, or competent they are, they are able to respond more fully to the needs at hand.

For one young woman, named Ann, the ability to let go of her own agenda meant she was able to listen and respond more faithfully to the movement of the Spirit in her life. Prayer and worship became lively and exciting times for her. She had always had a concern for social action, but now she felt a sense of solidarity and oneness with others in a way that was, at first, disconcerting. When she described her experiences she said that she inwardly sensed the pain, injustice, and brokenness of the world so deeply that she almost felt overwhelmed. She wondered how she could have been closed off from the woundedness of so many in our world. Her ministry flowed in two directions out of this new sensitivity and compassion. One direction was toward prayer. She experienced an inward oneness with Christ in carrying the world's hurt. She said she did not so much initiate prayers as give inward and outward voice to the prayers that Christ was already breathing at every place of hurt in the world. She was swept up in Christ's healing, emancipating, and redeeming work for all of creation. Ann's call to ministry also went in the direction of hands-on work. She said she felt an inward availability for God to use in carrying out Christ's healing work. She offered herself to God in prayer and actively asked her meeting where she was most needed. When I last spoke to her she was investigating work with a service and advocacy group dedicated to eradicating world hunger.

For some people, this deeper compassion includes awareness of their own needs, pain, and yearnings. In the darkness, they are able to move away from whatever has been blocking them from appropriate awareness of themselves as children of God. They are, at last, able to love themselves, care for their real needs, and respect what God was drawing forth from their lives. This is not a selfish preoccupation but rather a grateful response to God for the gift of new life. One young father said that in the darkness he found a grounding for his own life that was deeper than the sense of worthlessness he had inherited from his abused childhood. As a result, he was able to contribute to a happier and healthier home setting for his wife and their small children.

Forms of Ministry

The particular forms of ministry emerging from centeredness in God and interior freedom are as varied as the gifts and leadings of the individuals who have traveled this path. This array covers virtually all human possibilities. On one level the ministries of the dark night journeyer may be no different from those given to persons whom God has taken on other paths. The very nature of the dark night, however, gives the journeyer particular experience in two dimensions of the spiritual life which may become part of their service to others: spiritual nurture and prophetic ministry.

Spiritual Nurture Ministry—Dark night journeyers plumb the depths of the human condition; they learn how God works even in the midst of the deepest despair and suffering. In their struggles to let God re-pattern their lives and to learn a new way of knowing God, these journeyers often grow very sensitive to the movement of the Spirit in their own lives and the lives of others. They are good discerners; consequently, they may become excellent spiritual guides or nurturers for others, especially those who have had to face difficult situations of loss.

Prophetic Ministry—Because the journeyers have also come face to face with all the idols we use to prop up our lives, they may be in a good position to call us all back to God when we stray after the gods made with our own hands and hearts. They may perceive our social, economic, and even psychological idols before we do; hence, they can perform the function we see in the biblical prophet, calling

individuals and whole communities to accountability and
to complete trust in God's power rather than our own.

This role may be unexpected. There is a common
stereotype that people who have traveled the dark night
path of contemplation are interested only in the life of
personal prayer. Of course, such people are brought into
very deep levels of prayer; these journeyers, however, are
often the ones who have some of the deepest insights about
the functioning of the church-community and society at
large. They have faced not only personal places of unfaithfulness, but also corporate structures of unfaithfulness.
Their darkness has been a period for smashing all the idols
of unfaithfulness. From their dark night encounter with
God, they often bring a vision of a more faithful way of
living. Having been the iconoclasts who have broken the
old set of structures of the religious life, they are able to
return from that place beyond all images and forms to help
their communities give new form and substance to God's
call to faithful living today. (The "new" in this context
may also include the reclaiming of ancient forms and structures which the church can use in its attempt to live out
the meaning of faithfulness.)

The Quaker heritage has been blessed through the years
with a rich prophetic ministry. There are contemporary
Friends who continue in this tradition. Of course, there
are many people in all traditions who are led in this way.
For some it may mean an active involvement in social
justice, peace, or environmental work through secular or
religious agencies. For others, it means a leading to preach
God's call to righteousness and faithful living. For still
others, it means the ability to say a prophetic word within
the context of family life, work, and community affairs.
These people share many of the characteristics described

already: interior freedom to hear and respond to God's call and sensitivity to the needs to others.

In listening to a number of these people speak about the inward journeys that brought them to their ministry, I have been struck by two additional characteristics mentioned repeatedly. Both come out of times of darkness and stripping. One experience is the gift of clear-sightedness. This may be expressed in many ways and on many levels. It usually involves being able to see the patterns of life which have brought hurt and pain. These patterns may be in the wounding circumstances of childhood. They may be the social, economic, and political patterns which help to keep some nations in poverty while others reap riches. They may be the patterns of systematic insensitivity and discrimination in a community, company, or congregation. They may be the patterns of thought which blind us to the call of God. In each case, this clear-seeing became possible because of the reevaluation of all inherited patterns and structures that occurred in times of darkness. During these times all facades fell away. The persons took a stark look at reality. The experiences were sometimes shattering, but ultimately freeing. They lived through the death of an old world and were given the vision of a new world more clearly reflecting God's order. It is this clear-sighted vision which these people now bring to bear in their ministries.

Clear-sightedness is also an essential prerequisite for acknowledging the spiritual dangers that confront anyone engaged in this ministry. It is easy to fall victim to self-righteousness and arrogance while pointing out the failures of our socio-political, ecclesiastical, and economic orders. It is more likely still to find oneself accused of these faults unjustly by those who resent having their idolatry revealed. Those who have been in the dark night know their own frailty only too well. They can speak truth with compassion, not pride. They can respond with understanding to the anger of others because of memories of their own anger when they encountered God's stripping of their own idols. They can also keep fresh the call to renewed faithfulness which they have heard from God.

A second characteristic prophetic ministers mention is courage. Many of these people report that the major stumbling block for them in following God's call to prophetic witness was fear. They knew the inward dangers of pride and a judgmental attitude. They also knew the kind of response any critique of the established order is likely to receive. To persevere in this ministry, they knew they had to let go of much that they held dear: reputation, cultural measurements of success, job, and, in some cases, their lives. They also had to let go of less tangible, but very real, desires such as wanting to be liked and wanting always to be perfect, never making a mistake and, thus, never having to acknowledge their own human fallibility. For these people, the dark night was a time for confronting their fears in all of these areas. In this dark place, they found a new Center from and in which to understand their lives. Out of the darkness came a remarkable courage to speak Truth and not be paralyzed by fear.

Ministry as a Pattern of Living

The qualities of God–consciousness, oneness with Christ's self-emptying love, and interior freedom in those who have traveled in the dark night may engender more than a fine program of ministry. Of particular importance may be the ways or patterns of living which themselves are witnesses to God. Two special patterns may characterize those whom God has taken into the dark night, the way of silence and a life apart. Not all people who are drawn into the dark night live these modes of ministry. They are most likely to characterize people whose on-going spiritual life is expressed largely through the apophatic mode, rather than those who have experienced this mode primarily as a temporary or recurring dark night time of stripping and purification. These ministers can be tremendous gifts to the church and to the larger community. Very little is written about these two patterns of life and ministry; consequently, they are often misunderstood. A few words of interpretation may help us understand and appreciate the special qualities of this ministry.

Way of Silence—Through the centuries, the way of silence has marked the lives of people who travel the dark night or the apophatic path. We know quite a bit about the spiritual discipline of silence from those religious traditions which have developed its use into a whole way of life: e.g., monastic communities and Eastern Orthodox and Roman Catholic orders of hermits. Many people are not aware that there are followers of this path who are not in special communities; they live in our midst.

Silence for these people is a way of life and not just a mode of prayer and worship. When one is aware of the empty place where eternity touches time, silence may be the most eloquent response. These persons live in that awareness moment by moment. In a sense, they live an awareness of eschatological reality, now in time.

Silence is also a mark of humility for the human being

who stands in awe before God. In our assertive, self-fulfillment-oriented culture, we often forget that the tongue is the major expression of our human-centered will.

Silence is thus a very practical spiritual discipline for doing the deep work of discerning God's movement in our midst. It is easy in the rush of our busy lives, with all our plans and all our words, to receive so much interior and exterior noise that we cannot hear the Word that is spoken to us before all words. Those who choose, or are chosen by, the way of silence want to live in such a manner that they can hear the Word.

Much has been written in recent decades about the value of silence as a spiritual discipline. There is no need to praise its value again. But there is need to note the practical implications of a life lived according to this discipline.

Many of us take periodic times of retreat. We may have quiet days. We can understand silence as an occasional discipline. It is harder, however, to understand those who live the way of silence not as an occasional discipline but as a whole way of life. For most of us silence may be a complement to our usual way of living. For these people, silence is the primary way of life; speaking and activity become, in effect, the complement.

Some people who are drawn to the way of silence become monks or nuns, especially if they are members of church traditions which recognize such special vocations. Many Christian heritages, however, recognize no such special vocations. Even those churches which do have monastic forms of living discover that not everyone wishing to follow the way of silence would like to join a monastic order. Some people feel strongly that their vocation is to be a witness to God in the world.

These people can give our world a remarkable gift, if

we let them, but all too frequently they are made to feel ashamed of their way of life. A short while ago an exceptionally mature young woman from an evangelical Protestant church came to me to speak about the way God had been calling her to silence and prayer during the last few years. She had considered joining a contemplative community, but felt that this is not what God wanted her to do. Instead she felt led to mission work overseas. She had enrolled in a mission school where she was enjoying her studies and her life as a student. But there was one problem. No one understood or respected her desire for silence. She wanted to spend some time each day in her school's quiet room, but the room was always scheduled for meetings and activities. Paradoxically, there was not time to use it in quiet. Moreover, her school organized activities each day of the week and every night save one. There seemed to be no way a person who felt led to mission school and silence could find a way to do both. In classes she found herself in an awkward situation. She appreciated the lectures and the discussions. She was quite able to participate in them, both vocally and through listening. Very often she felt herself called to quiet reflection on what she heard rather than immediate vocal response; students and faculty, however, found her reaction strange.

Even the briefest conversation with this young woman revealed that she had unusual depth and caring. She was not ignoring the discussions or the people around her. Her silence was not the result of a psychological handicap. She conversed in an easy, relaxed way. It was simply that constant talking did not appear to her as the primary response required by God in all situations. She believed that constant talking missed a deeper reality. This young woman felt that she had something to contribute to the mission field both in her everyday work and in her silent listening and prayer. But she was beginning to wonder if her superiors and her colleagues would respect her way of living and ministering in the world.

In another case, a school, run by a religious body which historically had incorporated a great deal of silence in its life, was blessed with having on its staff two people who were drawn to silence as a way of life in the world. After a few months, the new head administrator took both people aside and told them how uncomfortable he was with their silence. He said he always wondered if their silence meant disapproval or antagonism. Both staff members were very gentle souls, who quite independently of one another found that faithfulness for them meant listening to the Spirit in every situation and speaking only when led to do so. They did not speak at staff gatherings very frequently, but when they did speak their remarks had great power and depth. Many staff members reported that the silent witness of their two colleagues helped the rest of the group come to a much deeper level in all their discussions. It was sad that the administrator did not understand the way of silence or the dark night journey which both people had traveled. As a result, he could not make use of the contributions which these two people were making to the school community. Instead he made them feel inadequate and inferior. It was also sad that the two staff members did not realize sooner that their way of life was misunderstood by some in the school community. They might have taken steps earlier to give an explanation to colleagues.

These examples are not rare. God calls a small but steady stream of people to the way of silence in the world. Most of these come by way of the dark night journey (although not all people come to this way of life from that pathway). The problem arises because even in church communities where one might expect to find people well-versed in Scripture, church history, and theology, few have had education in understanding the way of silence. As a result those who are led to this pathway find their ministry disregarded or actively disliked. We need to develop an appreciation for the ministry which these people can bring to the church and the larger society.

What are the possible contributions of people who keep the way of silence in the midst of the world? From their experience in the pathway of crucifixion and transformation, they bring an ability to endure the depths of human pain and see beyond to God. Through this ability, they have a word of life to bring to those who face serious illness, handicaps, death, oppression, and other traumatic experiences.

They bring a skill at discerning the movement of the Spirit which can help any group stay closer to the leadings of God. They may be good teachers of the spiritual arts. They often know much about the rhythms of being as well as doing. They know the flow and barriers in meditation, prayer, and worship.

Their quiet in the midst of conversation can slow down a discussion so that all participants can realize there is One who is present in our midst, if we will take the time to hear.

The silence of these people is often that of prayer, a prayer of listening, a prayer of intercession, a prayer of centering. Their presence can help others around them enter the way of contemplative knowing through which can emerge new creative solutions to difficulties. The ongoing silent prayer of these people upholds any group to which they belong. This prayer is often an invisible gift whose effect may be most noticeable when the people are absent and their prayers are missing.

All of these gifts are in addition to the other skills and talents such people may bring to whatever job, task, or subject is at hand. They have the same range of human qualifications as their colleagues in this regard. Because silence is a part of the ministry of these people does not mean that they are unable to speak, relate to others, or carry out the normal requirements of the workplace.

This list of gifts from those who live the way of silence does not imply that they are paragons of virtue. They may have few "natural" gifts. They may have many. They have bad days just as the rest of us do. They may suffer from the same anxieties and stresses. They have all the same human frailties. Theirs is not the only way to come to know God or express God's presence. It is simply that their life in silence is one gift that may help point us all toward God.

Those involved in the nurture of ministry must undertake the task of helping church-communities understand the ministry of silence in the world. They must also alert those living this ministry to the unfortunate reality that many do not yet understand this witness. Paradoxically, the silent ones may need to become teachers and speakers about the way of silence in those groups where they live and work.

A Life Apart—A second characteristic which marks the lives of those who have gone through the stripping of the dark night journey is a separation from the usual structures of the social order. This may happen by force of external circumstance such as death of a spouse, loss of a job, contracting a debilitating disease, the effects of political persecution, or social prejudice. For these people, the externally imposed separation from the usual social structures of society provides the outward framework of the dark night journey. But other people consciously choose to be in a position apart from the mainstream of society by remaining single, or maintaining voluntary poverty. Sometimes the line between choosing and being given this place apart is not a clear one. Whether originally chosen or simply given, this social position has profound spiritual implications for those who use their life situation as a spiritual discipline.

To understand the life apart it is helpful to have a more global or multicultural perspective than contemporary, mainstream North American society provides. As a culture we do not recognize the role or significance of people apart. But many other societies have not only recognized but honored such roles. The holy man or woman, the Russian Orthodox pilgrim, the medieval anchoress (e.g., Julian of Norwich), the consecrated virgin, the hermit on Mt. Athos, the Hindu *sannyasi,* and the monk or nun are all examples of people apart whose manner of life is acknowledged and respected by their communities.

These people are perceived as holy not because of any moral superiority, but because their pattern of life brings them to the place beyond the limitations of our ordinary social structures where they may encounter the intrusion of eternity into time. They experience something of that new order which is to come and not just the reality of our current human order. For this reason people apart have historically been seen as having a significant role to play within the community. They have been witnesses to that other world which is constantly trying to emerge into our world. Their witness could take prophetic form as well. They could give a critique of the prevailing social order and show how it did not live up to the principles of that eternal order. Precisely because they were apart from it, such people could see the imperfections of the prevailing social structure more clearly. One interesting example comes from contemporary India. Some Hindu *sannyasis,* those contemplatives who have abandoned all ties to this world and live a life of prayer and poverty, are among the foremost critics of the caste system in India. Some have returned to active work in the world to help create a new social order which is more in keeping with the vision they have seen in their contemplative lives apart from the world.

Anthropologists have suggested the term *liminal* to describe the role of people apart.[1] Liminal comes from the Latin word *limen,* which means threshold. It is the place "between" one social status and another or one "time" and another. Originally the term was applied to those people participating in a ritual, especially a rite of passage, e.g., those being initiated into adulthood. In many societies those to be initiated leave their childhood roles (their usual activities, sometimes even their customary clothing, their daily intercourse with family). Frequently, they leave their village and form an egalitarian community in the bush apart from normal society. There they are taught the sacred lore by the elders. They undergo an initiation ceremony. After this time apart the young people return to the village to assume their roles as responsible adults. A liminal time is one of leveling, emptying, and dying, to be followed by rebirth.

---

[1] See Victor Turner's discussion of the definition of liminal in "Liminality, Kabbalah, and the Media." *Religion* Vol. 15 (July 1985): 205-217.

Liminal states have two important dimensions.[2] One is an element of anti-structure which may become a prophetic critique of society. The other is a quality of limitlessness and unboundedness. The liminal state is one beyond all structures. All of these characteristics of liminality have parallels within the dark night journey and the larger apophatic path.

Many anthropologists recognize that the *sannyasi,* nun, and holy man occupy a kind of ongoing liminal state. They exist apart from family, caste, financial status, and other structures in the established social order. Their experience of life apart gives them the egalitarian value system which may be a challenge to the existing social order. Their attention to the sacred wisdom of their culture beckons to those within the old structure who are looking for deeper meaning. In a sense, what was originally a temporary liminal state has become a permanent part of the culture. That which is beyond all structure is brought into contact with the needs of everyday community life.

Various cultures have found diverse ways of establishing bridges to the world apart. In one East African society those men who have experienced a sense of closeness and free-spirited camaraderie that grew out of an extended period of disengagement preceding initiation can recapture that experience for brief periods in the adult workaday world.[3] For example, two men, one wealthy and one poor,

[2]Uri Almagor. "Long Time and Short Time: Ritual and Non-Ritual Liminality in an East African Age System." *Religion* Vol. 15 (July 1985): 219.

[3]Ibid, pp. 221-226

who come together to buy or sell a product may, by certain words and actions, indicate to each other that they wish to move out of these structured roles and experience again the friendship of the time of disengagement. They may step outside their present roles for a few minutes or a few hours to laugh and talk warmly with one another. Both the individuals and the society are enriched by the possibility of interaction outside of the limitations of social roles.

Christianity has had a long tradition of people apart. It has valued the ongoing liminal state. The monastic movement began to develop as early as the fourth century when Christian hermits left their homes, jobs, and wealth to live a life of prayer in the deserts of Egypt, Palestine, Arabia, and Persia. Sometimes the hermits lived alone. More frequently they lived in clusters with other like-minded people. These early hermits left the mainstream of society to find a deeper grounding for their lives. By remaining apart from the workaday structures of career and family they were able to gain a perspective on the social order which was not possible when they were swept up in its day-to-day demands. The hermits began to reflect on the true values of human existence. They wrestled with what was illusory and what was real. They grappled with questions of how to pray and to grow closer to God.

The success of their quest is attested to by the fact that great numbers of visitors came to the eremitical communities seeking spiritual guidance from the hermits. The hermits' lives were noted for their simplicity, hospitality, prayer, interior freedom, refusal to judge others, and radical trust in God. The witness of these eremitical communities is recorded in a collection called "Sayings from the Desert Fathers." (There were also desert mothers. This collection contains a few of their stories.) The "Sayings" are vignettes about the meaning of Christian life arising from the daily experience of the hermits. After a time of relative obscurity, the "Sayings" have again become well-known. Several paperback editions are in print (see bibliography).

Contemporary Christians find that they face many of the same questions as those early hermits. How does one find one's true self? How can we learn to see what is illusory and what is real? How do certain elements in our society's value structure block our ability to hear God's call? What does it mean to live a life of prayer? How can we find a firm foundation on which to build our lives?

The Protestant tradition has been wary of the value of monastic attempts to structure the religious life. Caution is in order. At certain points in Christian history monastic structures, which emphasized life apart from the main stream society, tended to denigrate the rightful place of faithful Christian living within the structures of family, job, and community. Along with this appropriate critique, however, a general bias against any "life apart" has sometimes become a built-in feature of Protestant thought. Some people assumed that the impulse to the eremitical life was itself completely illegitimate and artificial. They believed that this impulse was fostered only by church tradition and that it did not correspond to any deep movement of the Spirit in human lives. Spiritual nurturers can attest that this is not true. There is a small but steady stream of people whose path is in that eremitical style. A few join monastic communities or become professed hermits. Others are drawn to the eremitical way of life who know nothing about monks or hermits and who do not aspire to live in any formalized setting.

A broader historical perspective of the Christian heritage is, therefore, very helpful. It can enable us to recognize

God's call to a life apart when it comes to contemporary people. Those who answer the call can be assured that this liminal mode of life is part of an ancient and respected way of serving God and others.

The heart of all the visions of eremitical living is solitude. (Solitude in this context implies significant time alone, but it does not mean that there is no contact with other people.) As perceived by our this-worldly society, solitude is self-centered and escapist. But just the opposite has been true for its followers through the centuries. In its own way it functions to strip the person of self-centeredness just as does life in community. In community we have our rough edges smoothed by contact with others. In the give and take of everyday life we learn to give and receive love. The pathway beyond self-centeredness through solitude is different. In solitude we are at first thrown back on ourselves. We are then forced to face all those nagging questions about our lives which we usually manage to keep suppressed in the midst of our busy activities. Very quickly we discover that we cannot find satisfactory answers to those questions ourselves. Nor can we force God to answer our questions by diligently trying to use the "right" prayer technique or by engaging in multitudinous "holy" practices. It is then no longer possible to fool ourselves about the human ability to provide our own salvation.

In the solitude there is nothing to distract us from the painful realization that we are finite and cannot supply a grounding for ourselves. As layer after layer of self-illusion is stripped away, we face that interior empty place, the unknown beyond ourselves. In short, we enter the dark night. It is no accident that the apophatic tradition has been nurtured by those who stressed solitude and that those who were drawn to the apophatic pathway found solitude and silence their primary disciplines. Solitude grew (and still grows) naturally as part of the journey.

A life of solitude takes two shapes. One is that of actual physical solitude, i.e., time and space alone. It can come to the hermit in the hermitage, to the person confined to a hospital room, or to a prisoner in solitary confinement. There is a second kind of solitude, which often accompanies the first, but sometimes exists independently and can be equally as significant as actual time spent alone. This is the kind of solitude or apartness which comes simply from being separated from the usual structures of the social order.

For example, to live as a single (widowed, divorced) person in a world of couples and families is to feel the sense of apartness acutely. In some communities there is little way for single people to fit into the social activities of daily life that may revolve around children, parent-teacher associations, cub scout meetings, and get-togethers of neighborhood families. This isolation is sometimes made more intense by prejudice and discrimination. In the minds of many in our society, a single person simply does not have the same status, respect, or recognition as those who are married.

To be unemployed is to experience yet another expression of apartness. To be without a job is to be separated from the major social structures which provide a sense of self-worth and respect. While others go off to the workplace each day, the unemployed must stay at home, away from the centers where decisions are made, significant friendships formed, and much satisfaction and fulfillment experienced.

To be a person separated in these or other ways means that we are confronted with the realization that our society does not consider us persons of worth. The consequence may be a sense of meaninglessness, purposelessness, or partialness. We are brought to the place of emptiness and darkness which is the terrain of the dark night. But meaninglessness and partialness can be transformed. The "ordinary person" who is cut off from the social order in significant ways may encounter the same realities as the monk, nun, or hermit. In being denied fulfillment in and through the structures of the world, we may come to know a new way of appreciating human life which does not grow out of productivity, wealth, family, and power. By facing partialness on a human level, as a single (ill, unemployed, or otherwise set-apart) person, we may come to know a deeper wholeness that comes from relationship with God.

One must exercise care in speaking about the life apart. Obviously not all people who find themselves in a situation apart wish to be there. Many are victims of discrimination, illness, or bereavement. Our efforts should be dedicated to helping these people enter the fullness of our human society. Our prejudiced view that such people cannot be part of the mainstream needs to be challenged. Tough advocacy programs, laws to prevent discrimination, and the increasing diversification of modern society all have helped to ensure that previously left-out people are now being included in the life of the larger society. Handicapped children learn in ordinary classrooms. Ethnic, racial, and religious minorities have made at least some breakthroughs into the larger society. Single people lead full, satisfying lives independently of the old cultural expectations about marriage. Completeness should not be measured in terms of marriage, health, or any other culturally determined standard.

But some who walk the dark night journey find that the qualities of life apart have become part of their accepted, even chosen, way of life and ministry. They live into the implications of that apartness and solitude. They find pain on occasion, but they also find great depth and new meaning which would have been closed to them had they stayed within the usual social structure. Their gift in ministry comes from having walked the dark night path of solitude and separateness. Their very lives bring a critique of the partialness and limitations of all our human structures. We see, through them, that marriage, job, health, strength, wealth, or any other human measure is not an ultimate standard for deciding worth and meaning.

Many spiritual nurturers report that even though our culture gives very little recognition to those who live apart, people continue to choose this path. They may remain single. They may take part-time jobs so that they can be free from career demands for other patterns of living and being. It is striking that these patterns of life —singleness, part-time work (and a resultant life of relative poverty), and separation from the prevailing social structures—are precisely the norms outlined by the first Christian hermits for an eremitical lifestyle: celibacy, poverty, and solitude.

Contemporary followers of this path show us that it continues to have deep significance as a religious discipline and witness. The path is a way of letting go of those human supports which we may use as pretend gods. The mode of living which leads to separation from immediate fulfillment on the human level allows journeyers to be open to the One who encounters us in the midst of our emptiness and weakness. This path is one way to move closer to God. This is true to an extent even for people who could not consciously articulate the philosophical or religious significance of their way of life. It is true for people who originally stumbled into their pattern by some external circumstance not of their own choosing. By living into the structure and discipline of a life apart, they all have the same possibility of finding that their emptiness is transformed into God's overflowing fullness.

The literature of the monastic and eremitical movements provides numerous illustrations of the way a life apart has been lived in the past. We need to recognize the way life apart may be lived in our midst today. Two illustrations may help give a picture of the contemporary person apart. The first is a talented college professor who made the decision to leave a full-time position to assume a half-time teaching load so that her remaining time could be spent in quiet prayer and in nurturing her students in a deeper way than was possible through the academic structures of the university. Her colleagues thought her odd to make such a decision. This was not the way to climb the career ladder or to become a powerful figure in the university community. Her decision set her apart from them. The fact that she was divorced also left her separated from the family-oriented social structure in her residential neighborhood. Her way is lonely. But she feels at a deep level inside her that this is her calling, at least for the present.

The second example is a man who makes his living at odd jobs to support a lay ministry in his church. He is unmarried. He has an extraordinarily perceptive understanding of the function of the church-community and has helped many people, especially young people, to look beyond the individualistic values of our larger culture to the deeper values embedded in the life of the church. Most leaders in his congregation, however, overlook him because he has no degree; he is not married; his house is ramshackle; and he makes such "odd" choices about employment. (He prefers the poverty which results from his odd jobs. In this way he is free from the greater entanglement which would come with a professional career.) This man has traveled through a painful, yet powerful dark night which has led him to make his particular choices regarding ministry and pattern of living. Most other church members recognize none of this; they see him as a marginal person. He is, in fact, marginal in just the way the college professor is marginal in her community. The problem for both persons is that their communities do not understand the extraordinary spiritual implications of marginality or liminality in the lives of these two people.

Unfortunately, many of those drawn to a life apart are themselves unaware of the fullness of their vocations, because their churches have done nothing to help them understand what it means to be a person apart. Very often spiritual nurturers lack the training and experience to help dark night journeyers live out the implications of their path in ministry and pattern of living; consequently, journeyers have had to come to their ministry and their way of life entirely in the dark. Perhaps this darkness is appropriate accompaniment for such a choice, but it means that the persons who minister from this place apart are cut off from the human friendship, support, and understanding which all human beings need—including those who follow a dark night way. Little in the external culture sustains them. In their hearts they feel called to this way of life, but intellectually they have been given only *via moderna* categories to understand faithful Christian living. Others wonder what is wrong with those who choose to live apart since they seem to be going against the whole pattern of the larger society. These pressures make it very difficult for solitary persons to walk into the fullness of their ministry. They suffer, and their respective church-communities are denied the powerful ministry these people could give if they were accorded recognition and respect.

Perhaps more than ever in the past our society needs to perceive the link between the community and the person apart. Traditionally, the separation between the two has been stressed. Of course, separation is an integral element in being a person apart. But there is also an important tie which binds together the community and the person apart. Each has meaning in relation to the other. The ones apart are not just cut off from the world. Rather, these people are witnesses to another dimension of human life which comes from beyond all our socially created categories. This dimension is found when all the created world is stripped away and we face God in the darkness.

Persons apart may be the best prophetic witnesses in our society precisely because of their experience living on the margin. In turn, the community represents that place where God's infinite truth must take shape and form in our human world. While it is important to break open all that has become idolatrous, unfaithful, and oppressive in our social order, it is also important to live in God's order here and now, creating loving and just social structures which may emerge through faithful listening to God's Word. The ministries of silence and the way apart help make that faithful listening a reality in our midst.

8

The Role of the Spiritual Nurturer

A spiritual nurturer is a companion along the path toward deeper relationship with God. The goal of spiritual nurturing is to help the spiritual journeyer see more clearly how God is working in his or her life and, thereby, to respond more faithfully to God's call in daily living.

Spiritual nurturing takes place within the context of community, very often a community of faith (a meeting or congregation). Nurturing incorporates other communities as well, since we all belong to many human communities. School, work, neighborhood, and family may provide the settings in which nurture takes place. Nurturers may be family members, friends, colleagues on the job, campus ministers, hospital chaplains, or spiritual directors. Sometimes nurturing relationships may extend over years. In other situations dark night journeyers may seek out a caring friend or spiritual nurturer during a temporary period that is particularly bewildering or frightening. Nurturers may find that their work extends beyond relationships with individual journeyers. On occasion they are called on to interpret aspects of the dark night journey to particular communities or concerned groups.

The dark night journey presents two special challenges in the ministry of nurturing. First, inasmuch as the dark night is a time of intense inward and, sometimes, outward

stripping, the nurturer instinctively would like to do something to lessen the pain and suffering. This power, however,
is not in our hands, except in the limited ways described
below. The dark night, by definition, arises out of a process
of stripping and loss which is not under human control.
The nurturer cannot solve all the problems or take away
all the suffering found on this path. (Of course, if there
are things we, as nurturers, can do to make the journeyer
more comfortable, they are entirely in order.) Above all,
we need to trust that God is there in the midst of the
darkness and bewilderment. The work of the nurturer is
to help the journeyer move toward a closer and more
faithful relationship with God. This focus on the deepening
relationship with God differentiates this ministry from
related helping professions such as psychological counseling or medical therapy.

The second problem which confronts spiritual nurturers
who work with people in the dark night is the possibility
of being overwhelmed by the darkness and emptiness felt
by the journeyer. We may wish to withdraw and not have
to confront the painful places which exist in human life.
We know that we are vulnerable to the same pain and loss.
To travel with another in this path is to travel the path
ourselves. The only response to both problems is a radical
trust in God as protector and guide.

In certain eras of Christian history some writers on the
spiritual life described the process of spiritual formation
(i.e., the work of God shaping and transforming our lives)
in terms of clearly defined stages with qualifying characteristics attached to each stage. The work of spiritual nurture
consisted in helping people progress through these stages.
The spiritual director or guide, as the spiritual nurturer
was often called, was the expert in these stages and in the

work of God in human life. These formal models of religious growth contain a wealth of insight that is applicable to people of all times and places. Some contemporary spiritual nurturers have been schooled in these models and find them very useful. My own experience, however, is that God's relationship with each of us is unique. No one follows any single abstract model of spiritual formation completely. These models are best used as clusters of symbols and images which can help us to see what is happening in each individual situation. Nurturers are not so much directors as co-discerners of God's will. The ministry of nurture is not a task or program to be accomplished but a way of being with others.

The work of spiritual nurture does not require that we be experts in spirituality or theology, although all the experience we have trying to be faithful disciples ourselves and all that we know about the ways God works with people will be of enormous help in having a sympathetic understanding for others who are also trying to live faithful lives. When we recognize the dark night journey, either in our own lives or in the lives of others, we are better able to enter into relationship with other people as they go through a time of radical turning to God in the darkness. The main work of spiritual nurture is to point toward God. On the fundamental level we are all spiritual nurturers of each other. We can offer a listening ear to a friend, talk about a dilemma with a family member, or be part of an intentional spiritual-nurture or accountability group in our meeting or church.

Recognizing that we all have a responsibility to nurture one another, many meetings and congregations are encouraging members to form "spiritual friendships" or become "soul friends." Both terms refer to an intentional relationship between two people who would like to nurture and support one another as they try to hear and respond more fully to God. Soul friends meet together at regular times. They share what has been happening in their lives. This may include the ways God has been moving in their midst: calling them to deeper commitment, healing old wounds, and making them more sensitive to the needs of family and community. Spiritual friends often pray for each other. Sometimes they study or do devotional readings together. Above all, they are there for one another.

Those who have been in a spiritual friendship report that the process of talking out loud with one another about the central religious element of their lives often gives them a perspective they could not find on their own. These regular conversations become a spiritual discipline, helping each partner grow closer to God. They also function as one method of mutual accountability. If we have told our soul friend that we plan to spend fifteen minutes each day in meditative reading, in quiet openness before God, or in listening to a troubled neighbor, we know we will have to report on how well we have kept that intention. Perhaps even more important than these benefits, a spiritual friendship brings us the opportunity for learning to care for our friend. Together, we learn to trust God's healing and guiding presence in our lives.

Spiritual friendships do not meet all spiritual guidance needs. There are times when we find it very helpful to talk to another who is mature in the religious life and wise in the ways God works in and with us. Human problems and questions can be complex. An experienced nurturer may be a great help in these circumstances. Historically, many religious traditions have recognized, under a variety of names, those gifted in spiritual nurture or guidance.

Among Friends, both elders and recorded ministers exercised this function. Today, many meetings and church-communities are actively encouraging members who are led to this ministry. A number of fine training programs exist to help those in spiritual nurture work learn how to listen to the movement of the Spirit and how to enable others to hear and respond to the work of God in their own lives.

The images of the dark night described in this chapter are meant to be evocative, to open us to a way of seeing God's work which might be appropriate at certain times in our lives. They are not meant as prescriptions. In any particular situation nurturers should use the images or symbols that help point the way toward God. They should leave behind any images or descriptions which do not lead toward a closer relationship with God.

In the same way, the reflections that follow, on the role of spiritual nurture, are meant to open up possibilities, not define, limit, or prescribe. In every particular situation, adapt the ones that are most useful in helping others grow in relationship with God. Every spiritual nurture relationship unfolds out of the participants' personal histories, their gifts, and God's call to each. Nurturers must turn to God to learn how they may manifest this ministry with each person.

Among all the characteristics of spiritual nurture, three merit special attention: listening, interpretation, and guidance. Accounts from contemporary nurturers and journeyers in the dark night can help us explore these dimensions of nurturing. The names and certain external circumstances have been changed in these accounts to protect the identities of the people involved. While every individual's journey is unique, there are also universal characteristics in human experience. Widely different people may find that the same passage in Scripture speaks to them. They may have like reactions in similar circumstances. These similarities show us the commonality in our human condition. They help us learn from one another.

The Spiritual Nurturer as Listener

The spiritual nurturer is, above all else, a listener—to God, to another person, and to God through the other person.[1] The dark night can bring confusion, fear, anger, and longing. The nurturer, as listener, encourages the journeyer to share all that has been happening. In the process of sharing out loud, the journeyer can move through the shallows to the depths. The sharer can get below the surface turmoil and reactions to see what God is calling forth. This movement can happen in a number of ways. Our daily lives are often so busy that we do not have adequate time to "see" what is happening. We can be so occupied with our own activities that we allow no space for the Spirit to move. A spiritual nurturer helps create the space for the Spirit to move and for the journeyer to "see." Because the nurturer is listening to God through the journeyer, the journeyer may also be able to discern God in the midst of what had seemed only chaos.

Speaking aloud also allows us to name what is occurring in our lives. Without a name, a situation, movement, loss, or emotion remains inchoate. What is occurring may be

[1] I am indebted to Frances Taber from Pendle Hill for this outline of the three characteristics of listening in spiritual nurture ministry.

so close to us that we cannot reflect on it. Since we have no perspective on it, it can be overpowering. To name a condition is a very important step in our faithful response to God.

Listening, in a nurturing relationship, is not a passive activity. It requires the creation of a safe, confidential, and peaceful space for the one who is sharing. Listening also requires a prayerful atmosphere. The nurturer is not encouraging a process of self-centered introspection but rather a God-centered pathway of abundant and faithful living. Prayerfulness does not mean a formal, solemn atmosphere. The nurturer simply wishes the journeyer to become aware that there is another Listener in their midst.

The art of active listening also frequently includes asking questions and drawing out the sharer so that the spiritual journey can be seen in its fullness. Seeing the rich nuances of the story can help the naming process to go forward. Only at this point can the work of discernment begin.

The experiences of a Quaker seminary student named Mark illustrate the significance of listening in the ministry of spiritual nurture. Mark underwent a conversion process over several months during the early years of his seminary training. It occurred after a number of years of inward searching. He had lost his childhood faith and after much struggle finally came to a mature commitment to Christ. His new-found personal relationship with Jesus gave his life a sense of meaning and purpose. Mark offered up his life to God and the church through service in ministry. Shortly after making this commitment Mark became very ill and had to drop out of seminary. He was devastated. He said he felt as though God had slapped him in the face. His new-found meaning and all his life plans seemed dashed to pieces around him.

A caring nurturer in Mark's home meeting was able to invite Mark to talk out his feelings of anger, loss, and non-comprehension. In Mark's account the nurturer recognized many elements of the dark night journey. Because Mark had been a seminary student and was interested in the classical literature of Christian spirituality, the nurturer suggested he read John of the Cross's *Dark Night of the Soul*. Mark found the book very helpful. He felt that the description of the dark night matched his own experience during his illness. Over several months, through conversations with the nurturer, something deep inside Mark began to open. He recognized that although he had made a commitment to God at the time of his initial conversion, there was a deeper conversion that still needed to occur. He realized that he was angry with God for his illness because the illness stripped him of his way of measuring himself. He was used to demonstrating his worth to himself, as well as to others, by the things he could accomplish. After his conversion he had been willing to put his desire for accomplishment at the disposal of God and the church. He had been very active in his meeting at school, especially in peace work. He had done tutoring in the local inner-city high school. He tried to be diligent in his seminary studies. Mark had seen all of this activity as a sign of his newly committed life; hence, his anger over the loss of these activities.

Now, after quiet reflection, Mark felt that God was asking him to undergo a deeper conversion by acknowledging to himself that his worth, as a person, was not dependent on his own accomplishment. He had worth because God loved him. Because of God's love all people are endowed with the same worth. Suddenly Mark realized that meaning had not left his life because he had had to leave the seminary and give up his activities. Meaning grew out of his relationship with God. Nothing could destroy that relationship, not death, life, principalities, or powers. Romans 8:38-39 became Mark's favorite Scripture passage during this time. Mark felt God took him to a deeper level in the process of his conversion and commitment. He told his spiritual nurturer that he had come to know God in a way that transcended the experience of God's presence in the midst of his many former activities (as significant as that had been for him). God's presence now was not tied to Mark's sense of accomplishment. Mark thought that the stripping away of his centeredness on his own activity, which occurred during his illness, allowed God to carry out in him an inward preparation for ministry that went far beyond what he could learn in his studies. He felt that he was finally beginning to understand what the Christian faith was all about.

Mark was very grateful to God when he recovered his health a few months later. He went on to graduate from seminary and become a minister. When he went to his first church (a part of the programmed branch of the Society of Friends), he was excited about the possibility of helping the congregation grow spiritually in the ways that he had begun to glimpse in his studies and in his own life.

But things did not go as smoothly and joyously as Mark had anticipated. At his first church gathering he found himself in an argument with a long-term member over the rightful attitude of the Christian toward war. Mark had extensive experience in peace work. Coming from one of the historic peace churches, he had assumed that church members would agree with his understanding that peacemaking was at the heart of the Gospel. He was shocked to find that there were people in the meeting who not only did not agree about the significance of the peace witness in their own personal lives but did not agree that the Society of Friends had ever had an historical tradition of concern for peace.

This was only the beginning of Mark's problems. He discovered that this congregation included people who disagreed with him on a number of fundamental issues of faith. These were all issues which he had learned in seminary to be part of the church's understanding of the Christian faith. He was inwardly very angry at these people for not living up to his seminary model of the faithful church-community. He was shocked himself at how despairing he felt about this situation. The same sense of emptiness that had overcome him during his time of illness returned again.

Mark recognized he had a significant problem. He was fortunate enough to belong to a small group of pastors who met together in a spiritual-nurture group. Mark explained his dilemma to the group. No one attempted to give him any advice. The group simply provided the space for Mark to talk about his anger, fears, and dreams for the future. Mark explained how shaken he felt by his confrontation with what he perceived to be the unfaithfulness of his church-community. He said that in some way his letting go of his self-centered view of his own worth in his seminary days had only allowed him to pin his idealistic dreams onto his vision of the church.

In the course of talking about his predicament, Mark quickly came to a recognition of two realities: (1) The church did have a serious problem in understanding the fullness of the Christian faith. (2) He, Mark, had a more serious problem. He was starting from a place of anger in his ministry because the members of the congregation were thwarting his dreams of the faithful church. With extraordinary frankness Mark admitted to the group that he seemed able to extend his love only to those who agreed with him. Mark acknowledged his repentance for putting his focus on his dream instead of on God and on God's actual work in the congregation. He connected what was happening to him now with the previous period of stripping and re-patterning. He felt there was more within him that needed to be transformed by God. After prayer and reflection Mark told the spiritual nurture group that he thought God was asking him to be silent for a year. Mark did not mean that he felt he should not speak at all. He meant that God was asking him to take a time of deep inward listening to those in his congregation, rather than attempting to persuade them to undertake his program and ideas. Mark recognized that he was still tripping over his own needs and projections in his work with the church members. In the prayerful, listening environment created by his nurture group, Mark could hear God calling him to listen more carefully to those in his congregation and to discern where God was at work in their midst.

Mark returned to his meeting. Although he carried out his normal duties, he did not try to "reform" the community. He took special care, instead, to get to know and understand those people in the church who seemed most different from himself. He continued to report to the spiritual nurture group from time to time on what was happening. He himself was amazed at what unfolded. Those people who had seemed to him as the most recalcitrant and wrong-headed began to emerge as human beings with their own hopes and dreams. He learned about their personal histories, their fears, and their joys. More than that, he recognized that God was at work calling them to new life just as God was at work in his own life. In a very short time, he grew to love these people.

By the end of the special year of listening, Mark came to his ministry with an entirely new attitude. He watched where God was at work bringing healing, challenge, comfort, and direction to the community. With meeting members he tried to nurture and to respond faithfully to that work. Not surprisingly, even with all the weaknesses and inadequacies of the congregation, people began to sense new life. Something about Mark's way of listening to God through their lives was contagious. They began to see Christ as a living shepherd in their midst. Little by little, some of the husks and hard exteriors began to open as people listened to one another and to the Spirit.

Mark told his nurture group that God had taken him through these dark times until he could finally be centered in Christ rather than himself. Mark's experiences with spiritual nurture had provided times where Mark could listen more deeply. This listening allowed Mark to say yes to the work of re-patterning which God was doing in his life. It allowed him to move into his ministry with greater maturity and a deeper commitment to God. Mark's experience of corporate listening in the small nurture group was important in helping Mark understand the way listening to God could be practiced in his congregation.

The Spiritual Nurturer as Interpreter

A spiritual nurturer is first and foremost a listener. Out of the listening may arise an understanding of how God is working in the life of the dark night journeyer. Themes may emerge. Patterns may become clear.

Journeyers are searching for understanding, too. Since the dark night is so unlike what most people have experienced in their religious lives in the past, the search for understanding can be difficult. Nurturers may be able to help in the struggle to understand and respond to God. In the story of Mark, the spiritual nurturer recommended that Mark read John of the Cross. Mark found that very helpful. Many people, however, would not be ready to tackle John's sixteenth-century mystical language. Nurturers may begin by encouraging people to see the patterns in their own lives. If they feel it is appropriate, they may talk about the basic themes of the dark night journey in language that is more accessible for twentieth-century people. This kind of interpretation is never meant as an explanation for journeyers, but only as the presentation of an evocative image that might help journeyers to see the particular patterns in their own lives.

A spiritual nurturer named Maria, who has done substantial spiritual nurture work in her inner city, ethnic neighborhood, described one situation where interpretation played a very prominent role. Maria was a member of an urban Friends meeting. She kept a quiet corner of her old-fashioned parlor available for anyone who wanted to come and talk. One day a young woman named Teresa appeared unexpectedly at her door. She had had surgery for a brain tumor. The operation had left her physically weak and with several disabilities. Unfortunately, the doctors were unsure whether she was completely cured. This experience initiated a major inward searching in Teresa's life. She was re-thinking her religious beliefs and finding her relationship with God becoming more alive and personal. She felt God was asking her to a deeper surrender of her life. Teresa, who was a refugee, wanted to visit her mother in her homeland to talk over all that had been happening to her. But just as she planned to go, she got word that her mother had died in an incident in her country's civil strife. Teresa was devastated. Her own serious illness and her mother's death confronted her with her own vulnerability and mortality. The more she clung to her own preservation, the more she feared her own self-centeredness. She became terrified of God's call to surrender. In her mind it brought up fears of her illness and of death. She knew consciously that the surrender that God was asking of her had to do with a new centeredness on God rather than on human strength. But her fears about death and her resistance to God's call in her life were all intertwined. Her terror was manifested in nightmares and waking dreams. In these dreams she experienced her body spontaneously exploding into flame. Her experiences seemed so extreme in her own eyes that she wondered whether she was going insane.

These horrible experiences brought Teresa, in desperation, to Maria's door. She told Maria that she repeatedly pictured her own physical death. She wondered whether this is what God required of her; she was ready to say yes to God, if this was necessary.

Maria listened to all that Teresa poured out about her bereavement, her fears, and her sense of God's inward work in her life. She recognized that medical, psychological, and religious factors were part of the mosaic. Every spiritual nurturer should have a sense of when and how to intertwine spiritual nurture and medical or psychological aid. Those who do a substantial amount of spiritual nurture work often find it helpful to be in touch with a Christian psychological counselor who can give advice to them in their nurture work. A counselor who understands the spiritual journey can also be of enormous help to some dark night journeyers. Maria felt that the focus of spiritual nurture might provide a way of seeing what was happening in her life that Teresa could not find through her medical doctor or with the hospital social worker.

Maria had worked with a number of people who had traveled the dark night path. She had seen people paralyzed by terror. She recognized that the symbolic confrontation with death which Teresa described was not as unusual as we might think. Maria had found that spiritual nurturers can provide a great service by keeping close to the journeyers during this time, not because the threat of suicidal action is very likely, but because the pain and terror of these symbolic confrontations can be excruciating. A listening ear can be very helpful. It is usually very hard for journeyers to talk about this aspect of their experience. Their experiences seem bizarre, according to the norms of modern, rational cultures. They wonder if they are going crazy. The nurturer can give the journeyer a sense of respect and also an assurance that their words will be held in confidence.

For some journeyers, just sharing their fears with another human being and being reassured about the transformational nature of the dark night journey is enough. Many people will not have talked with anyone about what is happening in their spiritual lives until they reach this point of symbolic confrontation with death. They may never have heard of the dark night journey. They may not have been able to conceptualize what is happening to them. Simply learning about the dark night may be sufficient for them.

Other people need to learn more about the mythic, non-rational level of human experience in order to deal with their interior symbolic world. Well-educated people in contemporary culture have often been given little information about this aspect of being human.

Many preliterate societies have community rituals (e.g., initiation rites) which provide participants with a symbolic way of moving from one stage of life to the next. Some of the images which appear in initiation rites or the rituals conducted by shamans are strikingly similar to the images which appear to persons in dark night journeys. These widespread rituals of death and rebirth allow individuals and whole groups to pass through death to new and deeper life without psychological and spiritual harm and without getting "lost" along the way. Our society has few such rituals and where they do exist (e.g., baptism) the starkness of the death and resurrection images are often blunted so that the rites are not used in ways which help people to come through the interior death which is taking place.

Some people, paralyzed by their symbolic confrontation with death, find it useful to read about death and rebirth rituals in other cultures. It helps them understand what is happening to them. But even more than that, the reading can in itself be a way of living, through the ritual, into the reality of the crucifixion and the gift of new life. The biblical account of Christ's death and resurrection provides a framework for the journeyer who is a Christian. Those who have not previously met the historical Christ in a living way may find that the Christian message takes on profound meaning for the first time as they recognize that they are participating in Christ's crucifixion.

When talking with someone who is caught in the midst of the terror of death, the spiritual nurturer may remind the person that God leads us through these experiences not out of disregard for our welfare, but just the opposite. Hard as it may be to realize at the moment, this is an exercise in love. The new life awaiting us on the other side of death is much more fulfilling than what we can experience or even imagine now.

With these insights from her experience working with people in the dark night, Maria decided to offer Teresa some ideas about how she might understand God's work in her life at this difficult time. She talked first about the experience of stripping and the way it can initiate a time of re-patterning our whole lives. Teresa responded immediately with a nod of the head. She began to talk about the events in her life through these dark night images. New meaning seemed to open for her as she talked. Maria felt that her inward intuition about offering these images was affirmed. The images had provided Teresa with a way to name what was happening to her. More importantly, Teresa could see a way to "be" in the midst of her pain, loss, and uncertainty. She could face the darkness and emptiness with faith that God was there.

Maria then talked about the symbolic forms our minds use to deal with ultimate concerns. The confrontation with death and the experience of rebirth may take symbolic form in our lives. Teresa thought right away about some of the religious rituals and folk traditions she had experienced as a child in her home village. Teresa was able to recognize that God was not asking for her physical death but that she was being asked to confront her deepest fears of death, of being alone, and of being incapacitated. She was also being confronted with a call to something deeper than her own life and health. She told Maria that she felt that she needed to pass through these fears if she was going to accept God's gift of new life. She said there was something in her that was holding her back from the total commitment God required.

Teresa decided to allow herself to live through the symbols which her mind and heart used to come to grips with the experience of death and rebirth. She said that she could not explain out loud all that these symbols meant, but they gathered up her whole being. So one night, alone in her bed, she went through several hours experiencing inwardly the sense of being burned away. More and more layers of her were consumed by the flames. Early in the morning, exhausted and still unsure where all this was leading, she rose and went to the shower. As the water cascaded down on her head she had a powerful sense of God's presence putting out the flames. She felt she had been cleansed of all that needed to be purified. In the flame-quenching water, Teresa experienced trust in God's power that allowed her to accept her own weakness, frailty, and mortality. She told Maria the next day that she felt she knew God in such an intimate relationship that nothing could separate her again. From that moment she felt as though she had been granted a new life. Teresa said that her experience of the flames made her feel as though she had lived through the Day of the Lord, as described in the record of Scripture: "But the day of the Lord will come like a thief in the night . . . and the elements will be dissolved with fire, and the earth and the works that are upon it will be burned up" (2 Peter 3:10). On the Day of the Lord the old world is swept away and a new heaven and earth are born.

Teresa went on to say that when she experienced the fire, she was not fully consumed. She was transformed and could enter God's new order. The words of Isaiah came to her while she was in the shower: "Fear not, for I have redeemed you; . . . When you walk through fire you shall not be burned, and the flame shall not consume you" (Isaiah 43:1,2).

She vowed inwardly to God that she would live her life henceforth as faithfully as she could. She believed her life had meaning now as a witness to God's love and transforming power. Although this experience was many years ago, it has remained the central turning point of her life. Its impact has not dulled.

It took Teresa several years to recover from most of the effects of her surgery. (The doctors finally said they considered her original condition cured.) Teresa went on to become a friend-in-need to people in her neighborhood. People in the most extreme emotional turmoil knew they could turn to Teresa. She would be willing to listen to their deepest problems and fears. She also worked with teenage mental patients. In situations where everyone else could see only hopelessness and emptiness, Teresa brought the hope that God's power could overcome all.

In Teresa's life, the spiritual nurturer's offer of interpretation was the key to being able to cooperate with God's re-patterning work in the midst of the dark night. Not all dark night journeys are as dramatic as Teresa's. The interpretive work of a spiritual nurturer follows the needs of the journeyer.

Richard's journey is a case in point. His dark night involved no exterior stripping such as illness or death. His experience dealt with his prayer and worship life. He was a Quaker in middle life, and a writer by occupation. He was very articulate with both the spoken and the written word. From the time of childhood on he had had a strong interest in the religious life and a close personal relationship with Christ. Because of his vibrant spiritual life and his skill with words many people in his meeting had turned to him over the years as a teacher about the inward life. Friends looked forward to his messages and vocal prayers in meeting for worship. He was an avid reader of Scripture and often was able to open the meaning of a biblical verse during worship in a way that spoke profoundly to the condition of others.

At a certain point Richard noticed that his personal prayer life was not as rich in images and reflections as it once had been. He no longer seemed to be given insights to share in the unprogrammed meeting for worship. He wondered briefly if something was wrong; perhaps he was not being as diligent in prayer and worship as he once had been; perhaps he should spend more time reading the Bible each day or writing in his journal. None of these analyses, however, seemed right to him. He was not unhappy about the change in his prayer life. While he did not have much discursive thought about God, he was content simply to "be" in relationship with God during the time of prayer.

His problem came when members of his meeting noticed the change and wondered what was wrong. They said they missed his messages in worship. Richard began to feel as if he were being unfaithful to his meeting. He went to a member of the ministry and counsel committee to talk about the problem. After listening to Richard describe his situation in detail, the ministry and counsel member suggested that Richard may have been moving into the mode of apophatic prayer or contemplative prayer which is a more relational style of prayer and does not include much analytical thinking about God. Richard had an inward sense of confirmation as soon as he heard about the apophatic mode of prayer in which the sense of emptiness may provide the way for a closer relationship with God. The ministry and counsel member's interpretation helped Richard accept the way God was leading him in worship. He gave up any thought of forcing himself into another mode of prayer.

As the weeks went on members of ministry and counsel (whose task it was to oversee the meeting for worship) noted that while Richard was not as active in vocal ministry, his centered presence in the meeting had the profound effect of drawing others to a deeper level of worship. Indeed, when Richard was absent, the meeting often felt unsettled. Richard's ministry of being in God's presence enriched the meeting in a new way. Richard's new form of ministry, which had initially created confusion and disapproval, came to be appreciated by the meeting.

This situation illustrates that spiritual nurturers may sometimes have a dual responsibility. First, they need to help those people who are moving in an apophatic pathway to understand God's work in their lives. Second, they sometimes need to help the larger community recognize the gifts of those who travel this pathway. In Richard's situation, a little time and experience were all that was necessary for the meeting to appreciate Richard's gift of quiet centering in God.

Some situations require more help. In the chapter entitled "Ministry Growing Out of the Dark Night," there is an account of two employees in a religious school whose dark night journeys gave them the gift of prayerful listening as part of their daily activity. Some members of the school community misunderstood their quiet witness. This school was fortunate to have in its midst a teacher who did a good deal of spiritual nurture work. He recognized the quiet listening ministry that can grow out of the dark night and the ongoing apophatic pathway. He also realized that many staff members did not understand the way of life of their two colleagues. He made no attempt to give any grand speeches about spiritual pathways. But he did make it a point to respond, in private, any time a person spoke about not comprehending these two staff members. He would briefly try to suggest a way to understand them better or remark about the way he felt their presence was a help to the entire community. In a short time, he found that a dramatic shift of attitude had happened in the school community. Virtually all of the staff members came to treasure their two colleagues who had seemed to be alien at first. The staff members found that their quiet listening brought the whole community to a place of greater caring for one another and to a deeper centeredness on the movement of the Spirit in their midst. The interpretive work of spiritual nurture can, thus, take many forms, both with individuals and entire communities.

The Spiritual Nurturer as Guide

There are occasions in spiritual nurture ministry when listening and interpretation are not sufficient to meet the needs of the dark night journeyer. These occasions require more active guidance from the nurturer. Offering guidance is always a sensitive matter. It is an awesome responsibility to offer advice to others about their relationship with God. Such an offer should come only after extensive listening to another's journey and much experience learning about the ways God works in our lives. Guidance arises in the context of co-discernment of the way God is asking the journeyer to take the next step in discipleship.

During certain historical eras and within some Christian traditions spiritual nurturers were automatically expected to give guidance and direction to their "directees." In our more egalitarian age many nurturers are reluctant to offer any advice at all. While the hierarchical model of spiritual direction may have had its authoritarian excesses, the egalitarian model of spiritual nurture in our era may err on the side of too much restraint. In many congregations, people literally plead for mature nurturers who can help them with significant questions. These church members often complain that no one is willing to take on responsibility to guide them in their journeys. As church-communities we often abandon our task of caring for one another and being accountable to each other. We need to be more active as mutual encouragers and discerners of God's will. We need to raise up mature people of faith who can be guides for those who find themselves in need of help.

In the broadest sense, listening and asking questions are themselves forms of guidance. Of course, interpretation may be a form of guidance. In addition, spiritual nurturers may suggest avenues to help journeyers grow closer to God or to discern God's will, e.g., keeping a journal, practicing a particular meditation, or making a retreat. In some situations even more active guidance is appropriate.

Meredith's account of her spiritual nurture work with Donna illustrates a more active use of guidance. In fact, Donna had come to her to ask for just this kind of help. Meredith was part of the team ministry in her congregation. She was recognized by the congregation as having special gifts in spiritual nurture.

Donna was in her late thirties. She had grown up in very sad circumstances. A number of her family members suffered from mental illness. As a child she had almost been murdered by her mentally ill brother. Several extended family members had committed suicide. Almost all were alcoholic. Donna had never received a warm sense of belonging or love. Virtually every direction she turned to look for healing, she found only pain and brokenness. Now as an adult she had the added burden of discovering that she had a serious, debilitating illness which had no cure. The illness left her with little energy or strength.

In the midst of this terrible situation, Donna had grown close to God. She told Meredith that she never understood how this happened. Her family never took her to church. They certainly never encouraged her religious interest, yet she felt God reaching out to her. Her journey had been almost entirely in the dark night mode, as one could easily imagine. She did not (and could not) find God in interpersonal relationships or in the joys of daily living. There was too much brokenness there. But God had moved in her life in the only way possible, through the darkness and stripping. Donna developed a deep life of inward prayer and of faith.

In some ways her journey was the reverse of what we usually expect in human development. This reversal is true for a number of dark night journeyers. Most of us find God first in the love of family and friends, through Scripture and church life, and in contact with nature. This makes up the matrix of our daily lives. Only as mature adults do we begin to differentiate between God and our sense of the presence of God in all these avenues of living. The dark night journey often initiates this distinction in our spiritual awareness. Donna had done the reverse. She had not been able to experience God through her family or friendships. She had found God through inward prayer. In fact, she was greatly skilled in various modes of prayer and contemplation. Her happiest times in adult life were several years spent in a hermitage in a small mining town in the mountains. The depth of her insights about the contemplative dimension of the spiritual life was remarkable. As time went on, however, she knew something was missing in her life. She decided to seek out two forms of help. She contacted a Christian psychological counselor to help her deal with her painful childhood memories and the wounded places left in her by her early family experience. She also sought out a spiritual nurturer, Meredith, to help her see where she had become blocked in her relationship with God.

Meredith began by listening to Donna speak of her journey, especially all the experiences of pain, loss, and brokenness. After a number of conversations, Meredith recognized, as did Donna herself, that Donna was facing several blocks in her spiritual life. One had to do, paradoxically, with her sense of her own sinfulness. Another related issue was her understanding of herself and of the role of "self" in our life with God. Finally, intertwined with the other two was her inability to recognize God in and through people, nature, or any part of the created world.

The problem of Donna's sense of her own sinfulness arose because Donna harbored considerable anger towards the family members who had neglected and ill-treated her for so many years. As she became more aware of that anger in her psychological counseling, she was overwhelmed by the depth of her emotion.

The counselor encouraged Donna to realize that she had to uncover her anger if she was ever to be whole. He made her aware that anger is a gift from God that points toward wholeness precisely because it shows us where we have been hurt.

Donna understood these things. She also felt that God was calling her to something beyond anger. She told

Meredith that she saw her years of clinging to her anger as a way of saying no to God's healing. Meredith let Donna express her repentance for clinging to her anger and her desire now to say yes to God's healing in her life. Then Meredith spoke about God's promise of forgiveness. She encouraged Donna to put God in the center of her vision rather than her own sense of sinfulness. She gently suggested that excessive focus on our own sinfulness is, paradoxically, one way of clinging to our old, wounded, and broken selves. Meredith told Donna not to be overly concerned about falling back into feelings of anger. She encouraged her to trust God to do the healing work and not worry about having to accomplish it through her own strength. Little by little, Donna was able to experience both God's forgiveness in her life and her own forgiveness of her family. She realized that the damage of her early family experience would never be erased; nevertheless she was no longer paralyzed by that experience. Her anger toward her family melted as she recognized their profound problems. As she accepted her own anger, she could recognize and forgive the anger and hurt that caused her relatives to act as they did.

Closely related to all of these psychological and spiritual dimensions of anger, forgiveness, and healing were broader questions about the meaning of self and the place of the material world in our life with God. Because Donna's background was so full of pain and brokenness, it was hard for her to experience God in and through everyday relationships and activities. She had been blocked from developing and integrating a healthy sense of herself into her life with God and other people. Donna had grown up thinking that God must not want her to have a full and vibrant life. She had found God only in silence and emptiness. She decided that she was meant to renounce the joys of friendship, family, love, and the pleasures of daily human life in order to find God. She was afraid she might lose God if she looked toward the positive aspects of a healthy life.

The counselor continued to help Donna unravel some of the psychological threads which caused these dilemmas. Meredith continued to focus on Donna's unfolding relationship with God.

One day when Donna was talking to Meredith about her inward experience of Christ, Meredith asked her whether she truly experienced the reality of the incarnation, the Word becoming flesh, in her own life. Donna said that she intellectually understood the idea that God became flesh in Christ Jesus and that, therefore, the Christian faith taught that God could be found in the midst of the human, earthy, material aspects of our lives. It was hard, however, for her to accept the full meaning of this truth in her life. Meredith assured her that it was often hard for all of us to live into the reality of this extraordinary truth.

She prayed with Donna that the fullness of the incarnation might be opened in Donna's experience. Then Meredith encouraged Donna to reflect on how and where God was actually working in Donna's life. She suggested to Donna that her dark night time might have been God's way of becoming a living power in her life; more than that, the dark night might have been a time of preparation for the birth of Christ in Donna's life. After all, God had brought her to the place where she was seeking help. It was now time for wholeness. God was not asking her to live a narrow cramped life. Jesus said, "I came that they may have life, and have it abundantly" (John 10:10b).

Donna acknowledged that God's presence in the midst of her emptiness and stripping had been the one thing that had saved her from suicide. She did believe that God's movement was now bringing her to a new place in her life. She wanted to walk into the new life with a healed sense of self. But it was so easy to become discouraged and to fall back into the old patterns of thinking. Every time she became discouraged, Meredith encouraged her to focus on Jesus' promise of abundant life.

Slowly Donna began to recognize new avenues of living that had not been present before. Meredith supported her when she tentatively wondered about following some of these new avenues: she went shopping with a neighbor and bought a bright new scarf; she joined a singing group; she went out to have ice cream with friends. These were joyful activities not only because of the shopping, singing, and ice cream but because of the wonderful gift of new friends. Donna had not had many close friends in her life. Donna realized that she was, indeed, being given an abundant new life. She was experiencing joy in the ordinary activities of daily life. She told Meredith that her dark night journey was a strange adventure. She had always thought she was being asked to give up life in the everyday world. Now she saw that God had been at work in her broken world not because God called her to be there but because God could show her love even in the midst of her very broken world. Donna felt she was now being asked to give up her woundedness and her one-sided ideas of how we experience God's work in our lives. This meant reclaiming the fullness of God's presence in creation. She felt as though Christ had been born anew in her life, redeeming the brokenness of the world.

One problem, however, remained—her illness. As Donna found a new life opening before her, the question of her illness became more perplexing. She had been able to accept it when she had felt that God did not want her to live a full life. But now she did not know what to think. How could her life have meaning? Her energy was so limited that she had at most three or four hours available for activities each day. She had to be quiet during the rest of the day. She wondered why God had brought her through the emotional healing process only to leave her with physical illness.

She asked Meredith for an answer. Meredith said she had no answer, but she did have a suggestion. She advised Donna to look for God's movement where she could see it in her life and not to concentrate on the places where she could not see. Donna tried to follow this advice.

Although the answer to her question remained in darkness, she did find a new perspective on her illness. Since Donna had to spend so much time in quiet, she practiced her traditional contemplative prayer. This immersion in prayer allowed her to radiate a sense of God's presence to those who met her. This fact astonished Donna since she felt so much darkness in her own life. Donna, nevertheless, found that a stream of people began to come to her door to ask for a time of sharing or prayer. Donna had a way of drawing visitors into a deeper relationship with God. Her own acquaintance with the depth of human sorrows allowed others to speak of their sorrows and find the promise of healing. In the quiet prayer she often shared with her visitors, Donna gave her friends an opportunity to perceive the relationship with God which was unfolding in their own lives. Donna came to recognize that God had used her wounded life and her contemplative journey to bring new life to others. Although she never had an answer to her question about "why," she rejoiced in her own emotional healing and accepted her present physical weakness, trusting God to lead her in whatever way she was meant to go. She told Meredith that her spiritual guidance was an important aid at several critical points in helping her to move toward greater maturity in her religious life and to enter into the ministry God had given her.

Conclusion

The spiritual nurture ministry is varied. Nurturing means listening with and through another for the movement of the Spirit. Nurturing means holding up God's promise of healing, wholeness, forgiveness, and reconciliation. Nurturing means challenging all that is unfaithful to God's call or blocks us from growing closer to God. Nurturing involves being the mediator of God's love by being a companion in the midst of joy and sorrow. Nurturing means enabling others to live into the ministry God is calling forth from each of them. Through all of these dimensions, the spiritual nurturer points toward God. Only God has the power to create, transform, and sustain us.

The ministry of spiritual nurture can be especially significant for those who travel in the dark night. The dark night is a rugged and difficult pathway. Its terrain is so alien to most journeyers that the way is bewildering. In the dark night we face the crucifixion of all our humanly based understandings and expectations as we move from centeredness in self to centeredness in God. This night journey marks the death of the false self which has lived closed up in itself, trapped by its own illusion, turned away from God, and therefore unable to love.

The spiritual nurturer may be able to help the journeyer see that the dark night may be a time of preparation for the birth of Christ in our lives. In fact, we may experience simultaneously Christ's birth and resurrection. With the death of the false self and the coming of Christ, we rise to new life given in and by God. The fears, sense of worthlessness, anger, compulsiveness—all those interior blocks which kept us from abundant life—now have lost the power to paralyze us. In Christ the very traits which may have been the occasion for sin and turning away from God are now redeemed. We use them in God's service. We are able to move freely toward deeper caring and prophetic witness in our daily living.

The spiritual nurturer can also help us to see that the dark night may be a community- or society-wide time of stripping which not only shatters that which is unfaithful in us as individuals but that which is unfaithful and idolatrous in our whole social order. The dark night prepares us to enter God's Promised Land. The dark night is a prelude to the emergence of God's new order in our midst, here and now.

In the dark night journey we become one with Christ; we are united in his death and resurrection. In Christ we participate in the redemption of the world and the birthing of God's new order.

There is only One Guide in the darkness. Spiritual nurturers help people turn toward this Guide. Ephesians 3:16-19 becomes the prayer of nurturers:

. . . that He may grant you . . .
to be empowered with strength in the inner self by His
   Spirit;
that through faith the Christ may dwell in your hearts,
that you may be rooted and grounded in love,
in order that you may have power to understand
      with all the saints
      what is the breadth, the length,
      the depth, and the height,
in fact to know the love of Christ which surpasses
   knowledge,
so that you may be filled up to the whole fulness of God.
                    (Revised Berkeley Version)

In the darkness and emptiness beyond all things, which
we experience in the dark night, there is joy at being filled
unto all the fullness of God and knowing the love of Christ
which surpasses all knowledge.

This prayer does not simply reflect a pious wish, but an
experienced reality which grows in our daily lives. As we
turn toward God in the darkness, we become rooted and
grounded in love. We become empowered with strength
in the inner self by Christ's Spirit. We become one in
Christ's love, a love that carries us to God and embraces
the whole world.

Bibliography

This annotated bibliography includes resources in three subject areas: spiritual life, spiritual nurture, and liminality. Resources in all these areas are so extensive that it is impossible to include all of the best material in a single compact list. These selections are a few of those that I have found helpful. They will provide a starting place for those who would like to explore in more depth some of the themes presented in this book.

Spiritual Life—Books and Essays

This section covers a number of spiritual life topics which expand or provide background for reflections in this book. These topics include: the dark night experience, apophatic and cataphatic pathways (some books emphasizing one; other books intertwining both paths), prayer, the monastic heritage and its meaning for contemporary daily life, spiritual disciplines, and patterns of spiritual formation.

Benson, Lewis. *Catholic Quakerism*.Philadelphia: Book and Publications Committee of Philadelphia Yearly Meeting of the Religious Society of Friends, 1983.

Two chapters in this book, "Quaker Understanding of Christian Ethics" and "Quaker Conception of Christian Community and Church Order," deal with central Quaker understandings of the church community (relationship with Christ, being a church of the cross, the meaning of gospel order, corporate obedience) which provide the theological grounding for the traditional Quaker emphasis on corporate spiritual formation.

Bloom, Anthony. *Beginning to Pray*. New York: Paulist Press, 1970.

Growing out of the Russian Orthodox tradition, this tiny volume is full of deep insights for beginners and long-time prayers alike. The chapter on the "Absence of God," a complement to dark night understandings of absence, and the reflections on prayer in silence are of special interest.

Boyer, Ernest, Jr. *Finding God At Home: Family Life As Spiritual Discipline*. San Francisco: Harper & Row, 1988.

The author wishes to balance the spiritual life materials available about "life on the edge" (i.e., materials drawing on monastic models of silence and solitude) with explorations of "life in the center" (i.e., spiritual life growing out of our daily life in the family).

Brinton, Howard H. *Quaker Journals: Varieties of Religious Experience Among Friends*. Wallingford: Pendle Hill Publications, 1972.

Drawing on his extensive reading of Quaker journals, Howard Brinton outlines the spiritual formation process as experienced by Friends. It draws on such Quaker emphases as the place of silence, the pattern of community life as nurturer, and the significance of leadings.

Carr, Anne E. *A Search for Wisdom and Spirit: Thomas Merton's Theology of Self.* Notre Dame: University of Notre Dame Press, 1988.

A theological exploration of Merton's writings about the contemplative search for the true self.

The Cloud of Unknowing. Available in many editions.

A fourteenth-century English classic on contemplative prayer.

Dent, Barbara. *My Only Friend Is Darkness: Living the Night of Faith*. Notre Dame: Ave Maria Press, 1988.

Arising from the author's personal experience, this book presents a wide array of images of the darkness and theological reflections on the dark night. The author draws heavily on her Roman Catholic heritage in her theological reflections.

Edwards, Tilden. *Living in the Presence: Disciplines for the Spiritual Heart.* San Francisco: Harper & Row, 1987.

Reflections and practical exercises covering an extraordinarily wide range of spiritual disciplines. Much of the material grows out of the author's extensive experience in spiritual formation work as the director of the Shalem Institute for Spiritual Formation in Washington, D.C.

Fittipaldi, Silvio. *How to Pray Always Without Always Praying.* Notre Dame: Fides/Claretian, 1978.

The author begins with the question of the early Christian hermits about how to pray always and gives a fresh and contemporary response. Included are chapters on "Prayer as Questioning" and "Prayer as Silence."

FitzGerald, Constance. "Impasse and Dark Night," *Living with Apocalypse: Spiritual Resources for Social Compassion.* Edited by Tilden Edwards. San Francisco: Harper & Row, 1984, pp. 93-116.

Creative application of the spiritual theology of John of the Cross to contemporary feminist concerns.

Foster, Richard J. *Celebration of Discipline: The Path to Spiritual Growth.* San Francisco: Harper & Row, 1977.

The author, an Evangelical Quaker, presents both personal and corporate disciplines. He includes such often-forgotten areas as service to others, confession, and simplicity.

Herman, Emma. *Creative Prayer.* London: J. Clarke, 1921.

This holistic and vibrant presentation incorporates such disparate aspects of prayer as discursive meditation on central Christian doctrines and silent prayer.

John of the Cross. *Dark Night of the Soul.* Available in many editions.

This work has become a classic in understanding the spiritual path through darkness, stripping, and the seeming absence of God.

Jones, Rufus, M. *The Later Periods of Quakerism,* vol. 1. Westport: Greenwood Press, 1970.

The chapter on "Quietism in the Society of Friends" is a remarkable outline of dark night and contemplative experiences among Friends in the so-called Quietist era. (The author does not always use contemplative terminology in presenting his analysis.) The chapter on "Growth of Organization and Discipline of Friends in the 18th Century" gives insight into the process of spiritual formation through meeting/community life.

Journals. These are a few of the Quaker journals which Rufus Jones found especially useful in his discussion of Quietism and which contain material on dark night and contemplative experiences. Available in many editions, perhaps with slightly differing titles, at libraries specializing in Quakerism and religious studies.

Life and Labors of Sarah Grubb
Memoirs of Rebecca Jones
Life of Catherine Phillips
Journal of Job Scott
Memoirs and Letters of Richard & Elizabeth Shackleton
Journal of the Life and Labours of Thomas Shillitoe
Journal of John Woolman

Kardong, Terrence. *The Benedictines*. Wilmington: Michael Glazier, 1988.

This book will be of special interest to those wishing to explore the role of the religious community as spiritual nurturer. The author, a Benedictine monk, offers an overview of Benedictine spirituality and history along with an understanding of St. Benedict's Rule. (Readers who would like to compare the use of the Rule with Quaker understandings of gospel order may check the entry in this bibliography under Taber.)

Keating, Thomas. *Open Mind, Open Heart: The Contemplative Dimension of the Gospel*. Amity: Amity House, 1986.

The author gives an overview of contemplative prayer in the Christian tradition and offers a method of centering prayer as a way of living into this contemplative experience.

Kelly, Thomas R. *Eternal Promise*. New York: Harper & Row, 1966.

_____. *A Testament of Devotion*. Biographical memoir by Douglas V. Steere. New York: Harper & Row, 1941.

These two collections of essays on the spiritual life include, respectively, two of this Quaker author's best-known pieces: "The Gathered Meeting" and "Holy Obedience."

Lawrence, Brother. *The Practice of the Presence of God*. Available in many editions.

The reflections of this seventeenth-century Carmelite, who was able to find God as easily in the midst of his busy kitchen work as he did in the chapel, have nurtured countless people during and after his own lifetime.

Llewelyn, Robert. *Prayer and Contemplation*. Rev. Ed. Oxford: SLG Press, c. 1975, publ. 1980 and 1985.

This Anglican author discusses petition, intercession, the divine office, the Jesus prayer, and contemplative prayer as understood in *The Cloud of Unknowing*.

May, Gerald G. *Will and Spirit: A Contemplative Psychology*. Cambridge: Harper & Row, 1982.

An exploration of human consciousness by a psychiatrist who has extensive background in spiritual formation work. The author provides a rich interpretive context for understanding the contemplative experience and the nature of formation in the contemplative pathway.

Meninger, William. *Ten-Twelve Monastery Road: A Spiritual Journey.* Petersham: St. Bede's Publications, 1989.

An intertwining of experience drawn from life in a Cistercian monastery with reflections about the spiritual journey as it applies to all people. The book includes a discussion of the contemplative understanding found in *The Cloud of Unknowing.*

Merton, Thomas. *Disputed Questions.* New York: Farrar, Straus & Giroux, 1960.

See particularly "Philosophy of Solitude," pp. 163–193, a superb exploration of the way of solitude as a spiritual path, and "Light in Darkness," pp. 194–203, an introduction to the paradoxical understanding of darkness in the writings of John of the Cross.

———. *New Seeds of Contemplation.* New York: New Directions Books, 1961.

Considered by many as Thomas Merton's best book on contemplation.

Nemeck, Francis Kelly, and Marie Theresa Coombs. *The Spiritual Journey: Critical Thresholds and Stages of Adult Spiritual Genesis.* Wilmington: Michael Glazier, 1987.

The authors present a very interesting outline of adult spiritual formation and growth based on the insights of John of the Cross and Teilhard de Chardin.

Nouwen, Henri J.M. *The Way of the Heart: Desert Spirituality and Contemporary Ministry.* New York: Seabury Press, 1981.

Nouwen reflects on the way the insights of the early desert hermits (on silence, solitude, and unceasing prayer) speak to our lives today.

Ochs, Carol. *Ascent to Joy: Transforming Deadness of Spirit.* Notre Dame: University of Notre Dame Press, 1986.

This writer, known for her writings on feminism, presents a very helpful book on deadness of spirit, despair, and loss. Her topic is not exactly the same as the darkness experienced in the dark night journey, but there are clearly overlapping elements. She draws on her Jewish heritage to discuss a cluster of insights which are not usually stressed in writings on the dark night.

Pennington, Basil M. *Centering Prayer: Renewing an Ancient Christian Prayer Form.* Garden City: Image Books, 1980.

Writing out of his Trappist experience and his study of contemplative prayer in the Christian heritage, Pennington presents the way of centering prayer.

"Sayings from the Desert Fathers."

Among the many editions available, the following two books have special merit. The introduction is very helpful in Thomas Merton's *The Wisdom of the Desert: Sayings from the Desert Fathers of the Fourth Century.* Trans. by Thomas Merton. New York: New Directions, 1960. Yushi Nomura has accompanied selected "Sayings" with Japanese brush and ink drawings in a very effective way in his book *Desert Wisdom: Sayings from the Desert Fathers.* Intro. by Henri J.M. Nouwen. Garden City: Image Books, 1984.

Senn, Frank C. (ed.). *Protestant Spiritual Traditions.* New York: Paulist Press, 1986.

A series of essays on the spiritual traditions of the Lutheran, Reformed, Anabaptist, Anglican, Puritan, Pietist, and Methodist heritages.

Shannon, William H. *Thomas Merton's Dark Path.* Rev. Ed. New York: Farrar, Straus & Giroux, 1987.

An analysis of Thomas Merton's life and thought within the context of the Christian apophatic heritage.

Steere, Douglas V. *Dimensions of Prayer.* New York: Women's Division of Christian Service, Board of Missions, The Methodist Church, 1962.

The author explores diverse aspects of prayer and provides a helpful way through many of the questions and perplexities which arise in the experience of those who pray or wish to pray. The section entitled "On Accepting the Forgiveness of God" is a little jewel.

_____ (ed.). *Quaker Spirituality: Selected Writings*. Introduction by Douglas V. Steere. Preface by Elizabeth Gray Vining. New York: Paulist Press, 1984.

The author gives an introduction to Quaker spirituality and presents excerpts from the writings of six Quaker leaders spanning the time from the beginning of the movement to the mid-twentieth century: George Fox, Isaac Penington, John Woolman, Caroline Stephen, Rufus Jones, and Thomas Kelly.

_____. *Together in Solitude*. New York: Crossroad, 1982.

This collection of the author's essays contains several writings dealing with themes of contemplation, mystical experience, and spiritual direction.

Taber, Frances. "School of the Spirit." *Shalem News,* vol. 11, No. 2 (June 1987): 3.

This is a short summary of a longer, unpublished paper, "Thoughts on Marriage, Family and Daily Life as a School of the Spirit," in which the Benedictine rule for life in community is related to the spiritual practice experienced by the author, who grew up in a Quaker home in a Conservative (Wilburite) Friends community.

de Waal, Esther. *Seeking God: The Way of St. Benedict.* Forewords by the Archbishop of Canterbury and the Cardinal Archbishop of Westminster. Glasgow: William Collins Sons & Co. Ltd., 1984 (first published in London by Fount Paperbacks in association with Faith Press, 1984).

The author, coming from the Anglican heritage, writes about Benedictine spirituality and the Benedictine Rule to show their relevance for all people, including those not in a monastic setting.

Williams, Rowan. *Christian Spirituality: A Theological History from the New Testament to Luther and John of the Cross.* Atlanta: John Knox Press, 1979.

A profound interpretive analysis of Christian spirituality which opens up the depths of God's work in human experience while acknowledging the Mystery that is beyond what we can know.

Spiritual Life—Short Articles

Many of the journals listed here are noted for the consistently high quality of their articles. Readers who keep up with new issues will be richly rewarded with articles on practical, pastoral applications of dark night understandings and related themes. (Please see, as well, the periodical titles under the Spiritual Nurture section of the bibliography.)

Chalfant, Arlyn Teresa. "A Love that Has Been Through the Fire." *Spiritual Life* (Fall 1987): 153-160.

Dent, Barbara. "Leaping Into the Abyss." *Spiritual Life* (Spring 1989): 36-47.

_____. "Twelve Dark Years: Cosmic Dusters, Glaciers, and the Void." *Desert Call* (Spring 1989): 19-21.

Doohan, Leonard. "Personal Fulfillment in the Life and System of John of the Cross." *Living Prayer* (Jan.-Feb. 1988): 28-32.

Gallagher, Joseph. "To a Friend with Aids." *Catholic Digest* (Jan. 1988): 113-121.

Howell, Patrick J. "Loneliness and the Paschal Mystery." *Spiritual Life* (Fall 1987): 161-169.

Lane, Ronald. "Creative Suffering: The Purgative Way." *Desert Call* (Spring 1988): 6-9.

Palmer, Parker J. "The Monastic Way to Church Renewal: Borne Again." *Desert Call* (Winter 1987): 7-10.

Spiritual Life—Tapes

In recent years there has been a profusion of retreat and conference presentations on the spiritual life which have been made available on tape. Here are just a few suggestions.

Culligan, Fr. Kevin. "The Anthropology of St. John of the Cross." Society of St. Paul, Canfield, Ohio: Alba House Cassettes, 1987.

A psychological view of the human person as found in *Ascent of Mount Carmel* and *Dark Night of the Soul*.

Dorgan, Sr. Margaret. "St. Thérèse of Lisieux: The Experience of Love and Mercy." Society of St. Paul, Canfield, Ohio: Alba House Cassettes, 1988.

The spirituality of Thérèse as grounded in the theological understandings of John of the Cross.

Jordan, Clarence. "Metamorphosis" and "Love Your Enemies" (one tape) are two of the talks drawn from parables and accounts in the New Testament by this well-known storyteller, Greek scholar, founder of Koinonia, and activist in the struggle for racial equality. Koinonia Records, Americus, Georgia.

Merton, Thomas. "Silence," "Spiritual Direction," "Solitude: Breaking the Heart," and many other talks given as daily lectures to novices at Gethsemani. Sound cassettes are available from Credence Cassettes.

Spiritual Nurture—Books

This listing represents a variety of religious traditions: Catholic, Episcopal, Mennonite, Methodist, Quaker, and others. Each tradition has its own favorite terms for the ministry of spiritual nurture. Spiritual direction, spiritual guidance, eldering, and spiritual friendship are a few of the terms used for various dimensions of nurture work.

Readings and tapes on the spiritual life may themselves be forms of spiritual guidance and nurture.

Barry, William A. and William J Connolly. *The Practice of Spiritual Direction*. New York: Seabury, 1982.

A discussion of spiritual direction growing out of the experience of the Jesuit tradition. Among other important elements it explores the dynamics of the relationship between the director and directee, ways of helping the directee to notice and share key interior facts with God in prayer, and criteria for evaluating religious experience.

Bownas, Samuel. *A Description of the Qualifications Necessary to a Gospel Minister: Advice to Ministers and Elders Among the People Called Quakers*. Philadelphia: Pendle Hill Publications and Tract Association of Friends, 1989.

This contemporary edition of a Quaker classic was originally written for elders who were engaged in nurturing vocal ministers in the Society of Friends. Bownas's work, however, has a broader application because he outlines a pattern of spiritual formation and provides insight and advice which apply to all people who wish to become more open and receptive to God's leadings in their lives.

Devers, Dorothy C. *Faithful Friendship*.Cincinnati: Forward
   Movement Publications, 1986.

   The author presents reflections, meditations on Scripture, and practical exercises for pairs of spiritual friends
   or small mission and support groups that would like the
   help of a formal plan around which to structure their
   mutual sharing and growth.

Dyckman, Katherine Marie and Patrick L. Carroll. *Inviting
   the Mystic, Supporting the Prophet: An Introduction to Spiritual
   Direction*. New York: Paulist Press, 1981.

   This guide for those called to spiritual direction work
   is especially helpful because of its recognition of both
   the mystical and prophetic dimensions of a life of faith.
   It includes chapters on decision making, problems in
   prayer and the specific tasks of directors.

Edwards, Tilden. *Spiritual Friend: Reclaiming the Gift of
   Spiritual Direction*. New York: Paulist Press, 1980.

   This introduction to spiritual direction begins with an
   historical overview of spiritual friendship, spiritual
   fathers and mothers, and one-to-one spiritual direction
   within the Christian tradition. It includes a section on
   apophatic and cataphatic pathways as well as a chapter
   on group direction.

Gatta, Julia. *Three Spiritual Directors for Our Time: Julian of
   Norwich, The Cloud of Unknowing, Walter Hilton*. Intro. by
   Kenneth Leech. Cambridge: Cowley, 1986.

The author, an Episcopal priest, provides a very helpful presentation of apophatic prayer in *The Cloud*, the major themes and insights in Julian's revelations, and Hilton's way of understanding emotion in relation to God's work in our lives.

Girzaitis, Laura. *Listening: A Response Ability.* Illustrated by Pat Ryan. Winona: St. Mary's College Press, 1972.

Large print, fine photographs, and appealing cartoon characters make this little book on various aspects of listening to one another and to God a pleasure to read and ponder.

Jones, Alan. *Exploring Spiritual Direction: An Essay on Christian Friendship.* New York: Seabury, 1982.

The author takes seriously the image of spiritual warfare as the context of our faith journey. He includes chapters on the relation between therapy and direction, spiritual direction as a work of imagination, and spiritual direction as a work of contemplation.

Jones, T. Canby (ed.). *The Power of the Lord Is Over All: The Pastoral Letters of George Fox.* Richmond: Friends United Press, 1989.

Along with excellent insights about the early Quaker movement, this edition of the epistles of the founder of the Society of Friends provides an in-depth look at the corporate spiritual nurture work of George Fox as he writes to communities of Friends and to Friends as a whole.

Lacey, Paul. *On Leading and Being Led*. Pendle Hill Pamphlet 264. Wallingford: Pendle Hill Publications, 1985.

Leadings from God provide the heart of the Quaker understanding of spiritual formation and are at the center of much of Quaker nurture ministry. Paul Lacey is an excellent interpreter of the Quaker tradition of being led by God.

Leech, Kenneth. *Soul Friend: The Practice of Christian Spirituality*. Introduction by Henri J.M. Nouwen. New York: Paulist Press, 1980.

The author presents the history of spiritual direction in different Christian traditions, its relationship to counseling and therapy, the importance of prayer, and an outline of significant prayer traditions within Christianity.

Martin, John R. *Ventures in Discipleship: A Handbook for Groups or Individuals*. Foreword by Howard A. Snyder. Scottdale: Herald Press, 1984.

The author offers a process of mutual discipling, support, and accountability which draws heavily on Anabaptist/Mennonite understandings of the role of the church-community as a nurturer. On a variety of theological, ethical, and spiritual life topics, the book presents biblical sources, Anabaptist writings, and practical exercises for use in a discipling group.

May, Gerald C. *Care of Mind, Care of Spirit: Psychiatric Dimensions of Spiritual Direction.* San Francisco: Harper & Row, 1982.

This book delineates clearly both the significant differences between psychiatry and spiritual direction and the important help which behavioral sciences can offer to those involved in spiritual direction work.

McGuire, Brian Patrick. *Friendship and Community: The Monastic Experience, 350-1250.* Cistercian Studies Series 95 Kalamazoo: Cistercian Publications, 1988.

This study begins with biblical and classical understandings of friendship and traces these threads as they unfold in variegated forms within the monastic tradition. The interplay of the potential spiritual dangers in human ties of friendship and the recognition of the positive role of spiritual friendship provide a depth often missing in discussions which incorporate only contemporary cultural understandings.

Nemeck, Francis Kelly and Marie Theresa Coombs. *The Way of Spiritual Direction.* Wilmington: Michael Glazier, 1985.

The authors put the ministry of spiritual direction within the context of listening. They discuss those attitudes and practices which enable or block listening. In an age when spiritual direction can become an undisciplined fad, the authors also offer sound advice about too readily assuming we are called to undertake this ministry or that yearning for a director is an adequate sign that God wishes us to have guidance in this form.

Neufelder, Jerome M. and Mary C. Coelho (eds.). *Writings on Spiritual Direction by Great Christian Masters*. New York: Seabury Press, 1982.

Written just before the general use of inclusive language might have suggested a different subtitle, this book presents a broad selection of short quotations from the Bible and a diverse array of women and men writers throughout Christian history. The selections are arranged by topic and cover many of the most important areas of spiritual nurture.

Penington, Isaac. *Letters of Isaac Penington*. Historical editions are available in many libraries specializing in Quakerism or religious studies.

Isaac Penington, seventeenth-century Friend, carried on an extensive ministry of spiritual nurture through correspondence. His insight and advice continue to speak both to those needing nurture and those offering a ministry of nurture.

Sommerfeldt, John R. (ed.). *Abba: Guides to Wholeness and Holiness East and West*. Cistercian Study Series 38. Kalamazoo: Cistercian Publications, 1982.

This series of papers was presented at a Symposium on Spiritual Fatherhood/Motherhood at the Abbey of New Clairvaux, Vina, California, 12-16 June, 1978. Topics included attitudes toward spiritual fatherhood/motherhood in the biblical tradition, the Christian heritage, and some eastern religions. The book is especially helpful for opening up a variety of models of spiritual nurture including group direction, spiritual father/mother as a model and mentor in the religious life, and formal one-to-one spiritual guidance.

Steere, Douglas V. *Gleanings, A Random Harvest: Selected Writings by Douglas V. Steere*. Nashville: Upper Room, 1986.

In this collection of Douglas Steere's essays are several related to the work of spiritual nurture. Two essays "On Listening to Another" deal, respectively, with: (1) listening to another in a spiritual nurture relationship and being listened into wholeness by God, and (2) listening in corporate unprogrammed worship. "Evelyn Underhill and the Mid-Life Transformation" is a description of spiritual formation at mid-life and of Baron von Hügel's spiritual nurture work with Underhill. "Mind Your Call, That's All in All" is an essay about the importance of God's leading and call in the religious life.

Wood, Peter. *Eldering*. Canadian Quaker Pamphlet 27. Argenta: Argenta Friends Press, 1987.

The pamphlet suggests that the traditional Quaker elder may be seen as a spiritual nurturer.

Spiritual Nurture—Articles

There are many resources on spiritual nurturing available through articles. Please note the titles of periodicals as well as the specific articles mentioned. These periodicals regularly carry articles on this topic and related themes.

"Giving Each Other a Hand: The Emergence of Spiritual Direction." *Praying* (March–April 1989.)

Most of this issue of the Catholic magazine *Praying* is devoted to short articles on spiritual direction. Included is an article on group models of direction.

Jones, Joseph R. "Do You Need a Spiritual Director? The Soul on Its Journey Can Benefit from a Companion." (Condensed from Crossroads Series.) *Catholic Digest* (June 1988): 100–104.

A fine introduction to spiritual nurture in a very short space.

Johnston, Fr. William. "All and Nothing: St. John of the Cross and the Christian-Buddhist Dialogue." *Carmelite Digest* Vol. 5, No. 1 (Winter 1990): 44–58.

A comparison of experience described in John of the Cross and Zen Buddhism with a special emphasis on the mystical tradition of the West. It is helpful for spiritual nurturers who are working with people in the "all and nothing" path.

Louf, Andri. "Humility and Obedience in Monastic Tradition." *Cistercian Studies* Vol. 18, No. 4 (1983): 261–282.

Although the discussion of humility and obedience is set in a monastic context, the insights apply to many settings. The author deals with the role of spiritual direction within the paradoxical context of a monk's idealism, the inevitable frustration of the ideal view of ourselves, the movement toward true humility and the openness to love, and the asceticism of weakness and concomitant turning to God. This article is best read by those with some experience in spiritual nurture or reflection on their own spiritual journey.

Martin, Thomas F. "On Not Getting in the Way: St. Augustine on Spiritual Direction." *Living Prayer* (March–April 1987): 20–23.

Drawing on Augustine's insights, the author stresses the importance of humility and avoiding the model of "the expert" in spiritual nurture work. Spiritual direction points people to Christ as the interior teacher.

"Preparing the Way of the Lord." *Weavings* Vol. 3, No. 6 (Nov./Dec. 1988).

This issue of *Weavings* (published by the Upper Room) is devoted to various aspects of spiritual formation. The diverse articles (e.g., on solitude, asceticism in daily life—through parenting, aging, confronting illness, and spiritual reading of Scripture) provide suggested avenues of spiritual nurture that help expand our usual ideas about nurture involving only formal relationships with a spiritual friend or guide.

Van Vurst, James. "Seeking the Will of God." *Spiritual Life* (Summer 1987), 71–80.

The author informally subtitles his article "It's not like finding the needle in the haystack; it is the haystack." Too often, suggests the author, we perceive God's will as an "it" which is separate from the matrix of our lives. Our life is so blended in relationship with God that God's will might better be seen, instead, as the haystack rather than the needle.

Liminality

Endress, Richard. "The Monastery as a Liminal Community." *American Benedictine Review* Vol. 26, No. 2 (July 1975): 142–58.

The author uses categories of liminality as descriptions of and prescriptions for monastic life. He sees the liminal monastic community as having an eschatological focus and a prophetic function in society.

Fisher, Duncan. "Liminality: The Vocation of the Church (I): The Desert Image in Early Christian Tradition." *Cistercian Studies* Vol. 24, No. 3 (1989): 181–204.

_____. "Liminality: The Vocation of the Church (II): The Desert Image in Early Medieval Monasticism." *Cistercian Studies* Vol. 25, No. 3 (1990): 188-218

Seeing liminality as a reflection of the nature of the early church as it anticipated the coming of God's heavenly kingdom, the author explores themes of liminality in the Exodus story, the portrait of Christ as the prophet in the wilderness (found in the Gospel of Mark), and monastic life as the reassertion of the lost liminal vocation of the church.

Religion Vol. 15 (July 1985).

The entire issue is devoted to a variety of articles on liminality in traditional societies and liminoid (or liminal-like) phenomena in modern societies.

Turner, Victor. *The Ritual Process: Structure and Anti-Structure.* Chicago: Aldine Publishing Co., 1969.

Turner's anthropological investigations of liminality include numerous examples from his work in African societies, interesting reflections on *communitas* (the radical egalitarian community which arises when status structures are absent), and explorations of attempts at permanent liminality (e.g., with the early Franciscans). The book also outlines a provocative series of binary oppositions between characteristics of liminality and status systems (e.g., simplicity/complexity, acceptance of suffering and pain/avoidance of suffering and pain, silence/speech, sacred instruction/technical knowledge).